the year 2000

edited by
John R.W. Stott

W Farwell 84

InterVarsity Press
Downers Grove
Illinois 60515

London Lectures in Contemporary Christianity

© *Institute of Contemporary Christianity 1983. Published in England under the title*
The Year 2000 A.D.

*Published in the United States of America by InterVarsity Press, Downers Grove, Illinois,
with permission from Marshall Morgan & Scott, England.*

*InterVarsity Press is the book-publishing division of Inter-Varsity Christian Fellowship,
a student movement active on campus at hundreds of universities, colleges
and schools of nursing. For information about local and regional activities, write
IVCF, 233 Langdon St., Madison, WI 53703.*

Cover illustration: Jerry Tiritilli

ISBN 0-87784-845-9

Printed in the United States of America

Library of Congress Cataloging in Publication Data
Main entry under title:

The Year 2000.

    Includes bibliographical references.
    1. Sociology, Christian–Addresses, essays, lectures.
*2. Church and social problems–Addresses, essays,
lectures.   3. Twenty-first century–Forecasts–
Addresses, essays, lectures.   I. Stott, John R. W.*
BT738.Y42   1983   261   83-12871
ISBN 0-87784-845-9

17	16	15	14	13	12	11	10	9	8	7	6	5	4	3	2	1
97	96	95	94	93	92	91	90	89	88	87	86	85	84	83		

Contents

118675

CAPITALISM SEPARATED
ECONOMICS FROM STEWARDSHIP
INDUSTRIAL REVOLUTION SEPARATED
TECHNOLOGY FROM ETHICS
CORPORATION SEPARATED
RIGHTS FROM RESPONSIBILITIES

Foreword

'Futurology', defined as 'the art or practice of making forecasts about future developments in science and technology and their effect upon society', is a comparatively new word. It is not found in the older, standard dictionaries; it seems to have been invented in the 1960s.

Not that peering into the future is new. We human beings are insatiably curious. We want to know about our personal future. So, on the sly if not in the open, some of us consult fortune-tellers or horoscopes. But our horizons are not restricted to ourselves. We like to gaze into the remote future, as we do into outer space. Books and films of science fiction fascinate us. Or we dream the more scientific (or pseudo-scientific) dreams of the evolutionist or the Marxist.

It was in 1967 that Herman Kahn, President of the Hudson Institute, and Anthony J. Weiner wrote their book with a title similar to this one's, namely *The Year 2000*, subtitled 'a framework for speculation on the next thirty-three years'. Their emphasis was on the accumulation of scientific and technological knowledge and on the kind of post-industrial society which would result. Their forecast of worldwide growth and affluence has proved mistaken, however, for they could not foresee the oil price shocks of 1974 and 1979 or the consequent economic recession. Their book is therefore an object lesson in the fallibility of forecasting.

Ronald Higgins' *The Seventh Enemy* (1978) is more realistic because it focuses on 'the human factor in the global crisis'. The first six 'enemies' which threaten the world are the population explosion, the food crisis, the scarcity of resources, environmental degradation, nuclear abuse and the unleashing of scientific technology. Grave as these 6 problems are, Ronald Higgins continues, they are not insoluble, provided that the seventh enemy can be overcome, namely man himself. For man remains his own worst enemy, especially because of his political inertia and his personal blindness. He needs a new self-awareness, a fresh vision, a reawakening of his moral and religious capabilities. Otherwise, we face at best a precarious muddling through from crisis to crisis, and at worst, as the other enemies converge, a total catastrophe.

In 1980 three significant futuristic books were published. The first was *North-South*, 'a programme for survival', the report of the independent, international commission chaired by Herr Willy Brandt. It is referred to several times in this book, and forms the main topic of chapter 3 by Donald Hay. So I will not comment on it here. The second was *The Global 2000 Report to the President*, subtitled 'entering the 21st century', commissioned by President Carter in 1977, but presented to (some have added 'and disregarded by') President Reagan. It concentrates on the economic issues raised by the trio of population, resources and environment, and claims to offer not a speculative prediction but a computer-based statistical projection, assuming that present trends continue. The problems are faced with candour: a world population by 2000 AD of over 6 billion people, five-sixths of whom will live in the South; enormous deforestation, with a consequent increase in deserts, decrease of fresh water supplies, and extinction of half a million species of animals and plants; and inconceivable urbanisation, with Mexico City as the most mighty megalopolis of 30 million inhabitants. Yet *The Global 2000 Report* is less alarmist than an earlier though similar book, the Club of Rome's *Limits to Growth* (1972). It issues a solemn warning, to be sure, but it also envisages the possibility both that 'revolutionary advances in technology' may come to the rescue and – more important still – that 'the nations of the world (may) act decisively to alter current trends'.

vi

The third book published in 1980 is not the work of a commission like the other two, but of the world's most famous futurologist, Alvin Toffler. Ten years after *Future Shock* (an expression he has added to everybody's vocabulary), *Third Wave* is even more radical in its concepts. Referring to the agricultural revolution of 10,000 years ago as the 'first wave' and to the industrial revolution of 300 years ago as the second, the 'third wave' is the revolution with which the new technology has already begun to engulf us. What Alvin Toffler envisages is more than what Soviet thinkers call 'STR' (scientific technological revolution) or what he himself calls 'the super-industrial society'; he predicts for human beings new ways of living, loving and working, a quantum leap forward, an altered consciousness, even a new civilisation. Moreover, he has no fear of this social upheaval, despite its changing values. It will be 'a genuinely new way of life based on diversified, renewable energy sources'. One senses his excitement as he develops his theme.

The reason I have mentioned these six books is not only that their subject matter overlaps with this book's, but also that they illustrate the spectrum of futurologists who range from the most gloomy doom-watchers to the most naive utopians. Despair and complacency are equally inapproriate in Christians, however. What we need, as J. S. Whale wrote several decades ago, is 'neither the easy optimism of the humanist, nor the dark pessimism of the cynic, but the radical realism of the Bible'. Perhaps the greatest contribution which Christians can make to the futurology debate is this unique perspective about mankind. We refuse to be deceived by utopic dreams, because we know that human beings are fallen and that an evil twist of self-centredness has warped our nature. But we equally refuse to give in or give up in hopelessness, because we know that human beings still bear the image of God, although it is distorted, and can be redeemed, renewed, even re-created through Christ.

The 1981 London Lectures in Contemporary

Handwritten annotations: AG. 10,000 — 1758 IND — 1950 INFO. NAIVE UTOPIAN GLOOMY DOOM-WATCHERS

Christianity[1] were given by men who share this outlook of biblical realism and hope. Their lectures, now written up for publication, throb with Christian conviction, and sometimes with passion. I am grateful to them for their willingness to revise their lectures in the light of readers' comments, to the readers for making them, and to Steve Ingraham, my former study assistant, for organizing the lectures.

There can be no doubt of the urgency of the questions raised in this book. Christians should be in the forefront of thought, debate and action. Three facts should stimulate us in this. First, we are not the helpless victims of circumstances. One of the distinctive characteristics of human beings, as Paulo Freire and others have argued, is that instead of history flowing over us, we are able (under God) to influence its course. We are responsible before God for the kind of society which develops; we can be, as Jesus commanded and expected, its salt and light.

Secondly, we are confidently looking forward to the personal return, in power and glory, of our Lord Jesus Christ, and this Christian hope strongly motivates us. Not that we should make the mistake in 2000 AD which many made in 1000 AD, and predict that date (or any other date) as marking his return, for we do not know when he will come. Nor should we make our expectation of his coming an excuse for social inaction. On the contrary, the eschatological vision of the new world of righteousness and peace, which Christ will usher in, shows us what kind of society pleases God, and therefore gives us a strong incentive to seek at least an approximation to it now.[2]

Thirdly, as we face the end of the second millenium since Christ, the hearts of most people around us are failing them for fear. It is not the lack of natural resources which is the chief problem, however, but the lack of spiritual and moral resources. Thinking people know that the problems facing us – bewildering in their number, magnitude and complexity – are beyond us. Only a return to the living God who created us, sustains us and can re-make us through Christ, and a recovery of the authentic Christian faith in its biblical fulness and contemporary relevance, can enable us, with confidence and without fear, to look forward to *the Year 2000 AD*

John R. W. Stott
Chairman of the London Lectures Committee
Director of the London Institute
August 1982

1. The London Lectures in Contemporary Christianity were founded in 1974 to promote Christian thinking about contemporary issues. They are delivered annually in association with the London Institute for Contemporary Christianity.
2. See *Evangelism and Social Responsibility, an Evangelical Commitment*, the report of an international consultation jointly sponsored by the World Evangelical Fellowship and the Lausanne Committee for World Evangelisation (Paternoster Press, 1982).

The Contributors

Dr. Ian Blair graduated at Oxford, obtained his PhD at Liverpool, and has pursued research at CERN (Geneva), the Rutherford Laboratory and AERE, Harwell, concentrating on particles and nuclear physics, and the properties of lunar material. Between 1974 and 1977 he was involved in energy studies and now works on the environmental problems associated with nuclear power. He has written about 80 papers for scientific journals, contributed to the recent Methodist study (although himself an Anglican) *Shaping Tomorrow*, and has had a popular book published, *The Taming of the Atom*. He is also interested in politics, being both a County Councillor and a Parliamentary Candidate.

Marshal of the Royal Air Force Lord Cameron, GCB, CBE, DSO, DFC. Having served during World War II in Fighter and Bomber Squadrons, Sir Neil Cameron had a distinguished career in the Royal Air Force in Britain, France and Germany, becoming Chief of the Air Staff and Air ADC to the Queen 1976–77, and Chief of the Defence Staff 1977–79. He is now Principal of King's College, London.

Sir Fred Catherwood graduated at Cambridge, qualified as a Chartered Accountant and then entered industry. At various times he has been Managing Director and/or Chief Executive of Richard Costain Ltd, British Aluminium Co Ltd and John Laing Ltd. He was knighted in 1971 after serving for 5 years as Director of the National Economic Development Council. Between 1974 and 1979 he was chairman first of the British Institute of Management and then of the British Overseas Trade Board. Since 1979 he has been a member of the European Parliament. He has written *The Christian in Industrial Society* (1964), *The Christian Citizen* (1969), *A Better Way* (1976) and *First Things First* (1979).

Professor Martin Harrison studied in Manchester, Oxford (where he obtained his DPhil) and Paris, lectured at Manchester University 1963–66, has been Professor and Head of Department of Politics at Keele University since 1966, and was also Deputy Vice Chancellor from 1978–81. As his books reveal, his principal research interests are British and French politics, for he has written *Trade Unions and the Labour Party Since 1945* and *Politics and Society in de Gaulle's France*. His other interests include radio and housing.

Mr Donald Hay has since 1970 been Fellow and Tutor in Economics, Jesus College, Oxford (Senior Tutor 1977–80) and University Lecturer in Economics. He has twice visited Brazil, in 1981 as Visiting Professor, Federal University of Minas, Gerais, Belo Horizonte. His publications include *A Christian Critique of Capitalism* (1975), *A Christian Critique of Socialism* (1982), and with D. J. Morris *Industrial Economics, Theory and Evidence* (1979).

The Reverend J. Andrew Kirk is an Anglican clergyman. Having studied in London and Cambridge, and served a curacy in North Finchley, he taught for twelve years in fellowship with the South American Missionary Society, at the Protestant Faculty of Theology, in Buenos Aires, Argentina. Returning to England in 1979, he worked at St Paul's Church, Robert Adam Street in London, and in 1981 became Associate Director of the London Institute for Contemporary Christianity and Theologian-Missioner of the Church Missionary Society. He is the author of *Liberation Theology: An Evangelical View From The Third World* (1979) and *Theology Encounters Revolution* (1980).

Dr Alan Kreider obtained his PhD at Harvard, whose University Press published his *English Chantries: The Road to Dissolution* (1979). Having taught History at Goshen College, Indiana, from 1968–74, Dr Kreider came to London to become Director of the London Mennonite Centre and Pastor of the Mennonite Fellowship in Highgate. He is also a part-time lecturer in Church History at the London Bible College, and co-convenor of the Shaftesbury Project's study group on 'War and Peace' since its founding in 1976. He contributed to the symposium *Is Revolution Change?* and to *The Lion Handbook of Church History*.

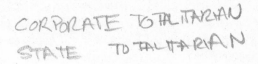

1 Human Rights: the Personal Debate

J. Andrew Kirk (*Associate Director of the London Institute for Contemporary Christianity, and Theologian Missioner of the Church Missionary Society*)

A well known campaigner for human rights, Amnesty International, which was founded in 1961, has as its symbol one solitary candle surrounded by barbed wire. It is an eloquent testimony to the human rights issue in the world today: a light and a flame kept burning in the midst of powerful forces that have little hesitation in snuffing out basic human liberties.

Amnesty International and other human rights organisations stand against the obliteration from memory of hundreds of thousands of human beings who are at the total mercy of one kind of arbitrary force or another. In particular it is the voice of the prisoners of conscience in over 100 countries, whose cries for justice and mercy are stifled by the padded cells of detention centres, prisons and psychiatric hospitals.

So effective, in many ways, has been this campaign that we are inclined to associate human rights immediately with the suspension of Habeas Corpus, imprisonment without trial, house arrests, deportation, physical assault and systematic torture. This is undoubtedly the dramatic side of the whole topic, brought all the more forcibly to our attention by the fact that Amnesty has concentrated its attention and efforts on a single issue, and has campaigned with obvious ideological impartiality.

There is, however, a cluster of issues concerning human rights which take us beyond the plight of dissidents in totalitarian societies, crucially important though their case

I

is. One of the first priorities for those concerned to think and act in the field of human rights is to discover as much as possible about what is happening and what is being said. I hope that in the following pages we may be able to explore both the less obvious and more controversial issues, as well as those publicised more widely.

I would like to begin by surveying briefly some of the current abuses of human rights; secondly, to look at some of the questions which they raise; thirdly, to examine the meaning of human rights from a Christian perspective; and finally, to consider the responsibilities of Christians in this area. I gladly acknowledge a heavy debt to a number of sources, some of which will be mentioned as we proceed.

Current Abuses of Human Rights

In Europe, the 1975 Helsinki 'Declaration on Security and Co-operation' has highlighted the granting and taking for granted of certain very specific rights. Since then there has been much bitter recrimination between East and West European nations over the implementation of the Agreement. In particular, Western governments and human rights organisations have drawn attention to such issues as the internment of dissidents in mental institutions, the continuing restriction of movement for individuals and families, the curtailing of the freedom of religion and, above all, the way in which the process of law is implemented. Thus, in the case of the Czech Charter 77 group, accusations of malpractice have either been extremely vague – 'acting against the interest of the State'[1] – or else totally tendentious – mental instability, homosexual practices and the like.

In Roumania a significant body of Church leaders has accused the authorities of discriminating against Christians over the pursuit of higher learning, salary scales, the suspension of pastors, the closing of church buildings and the dismissal of seminary students. In some cases pressure has been brought to bear on Christians to swear loyalty to the internal policy of the Communist party – this, in spite of the guarantees given in the Helsinki document of freedom of thought and conscience.[2]

Tony Chater, editor of the *Morning Star*, has said that the laws of slander against the State, and of anti-Soviet agitation 'constitute a serious limitation of democratic rights'. He goes on to argue that 'they encourage an attitude of conformism and inhibit the full expression of critical views even amongst supporters of the socialist system. . . . Truth does not need repression to establish its credentials'.[3]

Because of the long catalogue of abuses, a certain cynicism concerning the intentions of Communist countries has followed their signing of the Helsinki Agreement. At least until very recently the issue of human rights was placed at the centre of western diplomacy.

However, the nations of the West should be careful to heed the warning about the speck of dirt and the log. In manifesting righteous indignation against the practices of others, they may be blind to certain serious breaches of elementary rights themselves. Amnesty cites the case of new laws against terrorism in Italy under which people can be, and are, held for periods of up to 2½ years without trial, and in which new rules of evidence are heavily slanted against the defendant.

The right of conscientious objection in the West is not as openly recognised as it should be.[4] There is the case of the rights of migrant workers and the vexed question of immigration where many people believe (as in the new British Nationality Bill) that basic rights are being seriously compromised.[5] Others would argue persuasively that such activities as the indiscriminate sale of arms abroad, the export of riot-control technology and the training of the secret services of non-democratic regimes ('the repression trade')[6] all constitute a flouting of human rights.

More important in some ways than all these examples is the oft-repeated accusation by socialist societies that the

3

western economic system is incapable of guaranteeing some of the most basic rights of all: for example, the right to work, to decent accommodation, to protection against toxic chemicals and drugs, to equal opportunities in education, health care and leisure pursuits, to protection against the power of money to influence public opinion.

A recent programme of 'File on Four' (BBC Radio 4) focussed on the plight of Mexican American crop-pickers in the USA. Here are some of the facts which have come to light: 40 per cent are below the poverty line; life expectancy is 45, whilst the national average is 69; they are 25 times more prone to contract TB than other North Americans; half a million children, under 12, are working full-time; the school drop-out rate is 80 per cent, and the big food companies that employ them like Campbell's and Libby's fiercely oppose every move to establish the right of collective bargaining, being quite prepared to replace them with 'wetbacks', illegal immigrants, so-called because they enter the USA by swimming the Rio Grande.

There are other issues in human rights in the West which are not so well publicised, such as the right to receive and pass on certain classified information, the right of journalists to protect sources, the right not to have personal data stored in computerised filing-systems. There are yet other questions which, though more controversial, raise very profound concern about the protection of human dignity: should the death penalty be universally proscribed? Under what circumstances should the abortion of living fetuses be legalised?[7] What methods of physical coercion should the police be allowed to use? Do individuals in certain circumstances have the right to withhold or redirect taxes?

The list, of course, does not end there[8]. Consciousness of human rights has expanded enormously in the last two or three decades. Although there are cases of a silly fringe who campaign for human rights charters for every conceivable minority group and thus bring the subject into disrepute, on the whole the increase in awareness and the outrage against the persistent abuse and exploitation of human beings are enormous gains.

Questions Raised by the Abuse of Human Rights

At the Fifth Assembly of the World Council of Churches held in Nairobi in December 1975 an otherwise pedestrian set of meetings and debates suddenly sparked into life one afternoon when the issue of religious liberty in the USSR came to the floor. After some confusion and a heated exchange between delegates, which included the Metropolitan of Moscow, the debate was adjourned to the following day and an open hearing of the Conference Committee was arranged for the same evening.

During this subsequent very frank exchange of opinion the general policy of the WCC towards human rights in general was called into question. A former Dutch staff-worker of the WCC, Albert van den Heuval, accused the WCC of permitting what he called 'zones of silence', areas of the world where criticism of human rights abuse was deliberately limited. In the final debate on the issue he said that 'the acknowledgment that churches dare not be silent' was 'the great break through of the debate'.[9] Nevertheless, the final motion on religious freedom in Russia was exceedingly bland in comparison with the strongly worded and quite specific denunciations of abuses in Latin America and South Africa. There was widespread feeling that fear of a withdrawal of some Orthodox Churches from the WCC had prevented the zones of silence from becoming more than a hesitant whisper.

However, lest anyone is tempted to take up the first stone to cast at the WCC, it ought to be recognised that most people are implicitly guilty of what another commentator has called 'selective indignation'. Judging from the prayers of many Christians one would assume that the Church is harassed only in some Communist and Moslem countries. I have rarely heard prayers being offered for the persecuted Church in El Salvador, South Africa, Taiwan

5

or South Korea – all, significantly, within the western world's zone of influence.

Whilst recognising the different contexts in which humans rights are violated, even-handedness must be seen to be applied, or else the whole campaign falls into disrepute. As Paul Oestreicher says, human rights must not be devalued by using violations as a stick with which to beat one's political opponents, whilst excusing one's political friends. The policy of some western governments including, I suspect, our own is to take an uncompromisingly hard line against Communist regimes whilst excusing right-wing dictatorships of only temporary lapses from democracy. Such an approach, as is the case with Chile, [10] tells us more about the ideology and value-systems of the Western political policy makers than it does about the reality of the exercise of power in the countries concerned.

Christians especially, easily persuaded as we often are by the political propaganda thrown at us, need to cut through the superficial generalisations, prejudices and self-righteousness to which the human rights debate is prone. Let us beware, for example, that the crude denunciations of Communist agitation made about some Churches and Christian individuals courageously standing against massive and persistent violations do not involve breaking the ninth Commandment: 'you shall not bear false witness.'

This is doubly important because the victims of abuses are the powerless pawns of an international game in which ruthless men and women play out their understanding of life. Peter Berger, using as an illustration the Aztec and Mayan practice of offering human beings to the gods, likens the present situation in Latin America to these pyramids of sacrifice. Even-handedness in the struggle against human rights violations will probably mean being caught in a cross-fire of accusations about political meddling. However, as Paul Oestreicher says again: 'my own commitment is neither to liberalism, nor to Marxism, but to a curious idea put about by a carpenter turned dissident

6

preacher in Palestine that the test of our humanity is to be found in how we treat our enemies'.[11]

The selective indignation about which we are speaking and the defencelessness of those who fall foul of regimes which have made the rule of law into the servant of their own particular political philosophy highlight the extreme danger of power being exercised without checks and balances.

I find one of the most disturbing aspects of political life on a world scale to be the inability of authorities to admit errors. Humility, repentance, a modest assessment of one's achievements and failures are understood to be signs of gross political weakness. One may castigate the extreme mismanagement of an outgoing regime, defeated in an election or deposed by force, and promise a return to a system of open criticism and change. Soon, however, the insidious tendency of self-justification, of cover-ups, of alarmist exaggerations about the intentions of opposition groups creeps in, and human rights are again too easily laid to rest.

Holding power and exercising responsibility for the welfare of all citizens seem very uneasy bedfellows. Justification for suspending rights takes many forms. One of the most self-deluding is the appeal to national interests. These are defined as blanket concepts in terms of real, or imagined, threats to a particular way of life caused by ill-defined enemies of the nation concerned. The government in power chooses to declare these enemies, even when there is no evidence of any violent activity having been engaged in, to be subversive groups whose intention is to destabilise existing society. They can only be countered, so runs the well-worn argument, by defending law and order. It is on this basis that martial law or a state of emergency is declared and justified. Both Russia and the USA have used this kind of argument to justify direct or indirect involvement in the affairs of a nation they consider of strategic importance to their own interests. In this respect their foreign policy seems to be identical.

I am amazed how easily many Christians are persuaded to believe and support this argument for a policy of National Security. It does not, however, stand up to close examination. In the first place, it is based on the erroneous belief that the state is the authority that grants freedoms and rights to people. But nation and state are not synonymous entities. That is, the interests of the nation cannot be decided unilaterally by the executive power of the state; even less, when the government is not accountable in any way to an electorate. Any government which acts in an authoritarian manner has already confused might with right; it is only a small step to giving or withholding essential freedoms by arbitrary fiat. Secondly, the notion of law and order is not self-explanatory. It often means 'my law' and 'my order', used to defend my particular interests. In this way the rights of human beings are defined solely in relation to the power elite. In fact many 'national security' states have consistently flouted international codes of behaviour, and their laws have been denounced by such bodies as the International Court at The Hague and the International Association of Jurists. They might well be said to be upholding 'lawlessness' and 'disorder'.

The reason why the Church and the state in Latin America are often in conflict today is that the former appeals to an authority higher than that of the latter. It presses all governments to give an account of their stewardship of power before the judgment-seat of Jesus Christ. It stands usually as the only major body of opinion in society which refuses to be intimidated either by specious calls to national pride and unity or by the use of violence. At the same time, it provides an open space for dissent from the suffocating repression of totalitarian regimes. One of the most significant events of the last twenty years has been the way this role of the Church has grown in different parts of the world, though not without fierce internal opposition.

The Meaning of Human Rights

The Universal Declaration of Human Rights was signed on 16th Dec 1948. There were forty-eight votes in favour, none against. At the time all Eastern European countries, South Africa and Saudi Arabia significantly abstained. The thirty quite brief articles are ideals concerning the inherent dignity of every human being. They are held to be universally valid 'without any kind of distinction' based on 'race, colour, sex, language, religion, political opinion' or on 'national or social origin, wealth or birth'. In other words they are considered to be the *inalienable* rights of all people irrespective of cultural, ideological or religious beliefs.

The Declaration sounds magnificent. Its majestic and lofty sentiments contrasted starkly with the brutality and utter degradation of the war recently ended in Europe. However, its provisions have not remained totally undisputed.

Two major questions have arisen. The first concerns the intention of the Declaration. Is it a moral consensus with which the world community has already agreed, or a general aspiration to be fulfilled at some later date? Is it a charter which sets out maximum rights, or only minimum ones? Is the ideal model of society implied in the clauses a western-style democracy, some form of democratic socialism, or some other? To what extent should the rights be incorporated into legislation? Should the UN work towards a body which could enforce them around the globe, modelled perhaps on the Court of Human Rights in Strasbourg? These are not easy questions to answer, for the issue of human rights penetrates to the roots of what it means to be human. Thus, the second question has to do with the relationship between civil and political rights (the rights of individual citizens) and economic and social rights (the rights of societies as a whole to suspend some of the freedoms of individuals in order to secure the basic rights of the majority to life, health, education and shelter).

general aspiration
moral consensus INDIVIDUAL RIGHTS
SOCIAL RIGHTS

9

The socialist countries of Eastern Europe justified their abstention from signing the Declaration on the Marxist premise that rights are meaningful only within a particular kind of society, one where the economic base of society has been totally changed.[12] According to this argument human rights within a capitalist economy are based on high-sounding liberal ideals which, in reality, mask the inability of the system to guarantee the most fundamental rights of all: life, economic security, and personal development through an educational system that maintains equal standards for all.

However much propaganda advantage both sides of the divide wish to achieve, one thing is fairly clear today, namely that there is no nation that is willing to admit having suspended normal human rights guarantees. It either denies any knowledge of abuse or else goes to great lengths to justify temporary (a nice flexible word) curtailment. So there is almost universal agreement today that the protection of human rights is a good thing. Yet a pervading vagueness still remains that allows an enormous and quite unhealthy variety of practices. No other contemporary issue, I believe, poses so forcefully the question about the meaning of being human as that of human rights.

If ever there was an issue whose deep concerns a pluralistic, irreligious, pragmatic and hedonistic society like ours has such limited resources to answer, surely it is this one. Bishop John Austin Baker, in a paper on human rights, reminds us that in nature the notion of rights is a meaningless concept. So what makes human beings different from the animal world? He also points out that rights are based ultimately on the concept of the individual which in turn presumes the existence of personality. But from where do such ideas come, and on what kind of facts are they based? Historically and sociologically, they certainly have not always been (as the United States' Constitution confidently proclaims) 'self evidently true'.

Outside the biblical revelation of God, the meaning

of being human is entirely problematical. The liberal-humanist and Marxist traditions are in my estimation parasitical upon the ethical dynamism of the biblical message.

Left to themselves, without centuries of Christian teaching and experience to draw upon, they would wither away into either an evolutionary or an economic determinism.

In those cases, rights could be recognised only on the basis of promoting either the survival of the fittest, in which case the severely handicapped baby has no automatic right to curative medicine or surgery, or the coming of a classless society. The very highest ethic to which humanity has attained, when untouched by biblical faith, is the golden rule stated negatively, 'do not do to others what you would not want them to do to you'.

This might provide some basis for a minimum code of human rights. It is shaky ground, however, for it depends ultimately on self-interest and the imposition of restraint and discipline from within. Each individual would be an autonomous moral agent dependent on his own perceptions for guidance. It is difficult to see how such a narrowly conceived foundation could ever be universalised.

The biblical understanding of men and women created in the image of the God and Father of Jesus Christ, and called to the fulness of life in his kingdom, gives both a totally unique and wholly adequate framework in which to tackle the related questions of 'human' and 'rights'.

Of course, the solemn pronouncement of an ethic based on creation and on the kingdom does not settle every matter automatically. We soon discover, for example, that there is no biblical equivalent to the word 'right'. Some speculate that this may be due to the fact that humanity's revolt against God has meant a forfeiture of rights. I think, however, that there are other reasons. There is a sense in which it cannot be taken for granted that the creature possesses a set of inherent rights in the universe, for that would entail the existence of an absolute demand independent of God. Rights, if they exist, are given by the Creator. They depend, in biblical thinking, on the inescapable fact that God has bound himself to human beings; that, in spite of man's drive to rid himself of God, he has committed himself for all time to care for and liberate his special creation. Rights are granted both because of and in spite of man's sin. In a world of perfect moral righteousness human rights are superfluous, but in a fallen world some human beings need protecting against the lust and violence of others.

The drama of God's grace in involving himself totally in the filth and suffering of fallen human life emphasises the fact that rights are not the same thing as deserts. With respect to God, human beings deserve nothing. God has signed no contractual obligation to pay attention to mankind's claim, on the condition that he behaves himself. The notion of building up merit in order to put pressure on God is a wholly pagan view of religion.

God acts to protect and liberate because it is his nature to do so. The possibility of human rights, although often couched in the language of law, is ultimately bound up with the Gospel of God's free grace. As Bishop Baker says, 'all have forfeited rights before God, they are given back to all who are honest enough to recognise they have none. The negative golden rule then becomes something radically different: "do to others what you need God to do for you".'[13]

The question whether human beings possess inalienable rights towards one another still remains. Again the Bible comes up with a surprising answer; surprising, that is, to a world used to thinking and acting independently of any obligation to God. Rights are never conceived as a simple contract or convention between autonomous human beings, and even natural law is obliged to presuppose a Law-Giver. Such an idea would have seemed absurd to prophet and apostle. Biblically speaking, men and women have no final being or meaning apart from God. They are, therefore, under obligation to God *for* their fellow human beings, rather than *to* them. The whole concept of rights is changed into that of responsibilities. So rights are not what *we* deserve, but what *God* requires. They accord with God's righteousness.

Now God's righteousness is not an abstract, moral or philosophical idea; it has been demonstrated concretely within the life of society. During the time of Israel's stay in Egypt, God heard the cry of his people arising out of the extreme abuse of human dignity they were suffering. The Exodus was God's way of restoring a 'right' situation. It demonstrated that disaster will overtake all who flout what Amos calls 'the covenant of brotherhood' (1.9). The laws and institutions which God gave to Moses were designed to maintain the justice and righteousness on which the new life in the land of promise would be based. The ideal can be summed up in the word 'freedom', the very opposite of the bondage and subjugation which the people had experienced in Egypt. And freedom is expressed by that great and inclusive word *shalom* ('peace'): not only, nor primarily, in its negative aspect of an absence of threat from one's enemies, but in the positive sense of completeness, welfare, a measure of prosperity and harmony between communities. Shalom is a word which refers to a new kind of society. It is the ultimate human right, because God both demands its implementation, and promises to bring it about.

So, as rights are both given and guaranteed by God himself, they are neither a matter of charity, nor of concession to public opinion, but of justice. To refuse them is directly to oppose God.[14] This, incidentally, is the ultimate sanction.

In the light of the grace of God in and through Jesus Christ human rights take on a new dimension. Whereas the language of rights tends to focus on legal minima, the gospel of God's righteousness calls us to discover and practice new obligations to our fellow human beings. So, as Christopher Wright points out[15], in the Parable of the Good Samaritan the initial question, 'who is my neighbour?', i.e. 'who can be said to have well-defined rights upon my charity?' is turned into a very different one by Jesus: 'who proved to be neighbour to the Samaritan?' The love which Jesus commands ('go and do *likewise*') knows no frontiers.

According to the overall perspective of the biblical view of God and man it is invidious to speak of a 'hierarchy' of rights. In classifying rights, however, the tendency has been to focus on the negative aspects: what human beings should never do to one another. The positive rights are then considered in terms of long-term possibilities, rather than immediate necessities. In practice this means focusing the whole human rights debate on civil and political rights, whilst neglecting or postponing the economic and social ones. In this way our western societies, which undoubtedly have the best current record in terms of freedom from personal physical abuse, censorship and the suspension of the rule of law, are able to feel smugly complacent. At the same time they are blind to their complicity in a world economic order which makes the right to life itself in many places increasingly unattainable.

The so-called North-South dialogue emphasises the distinctions to which we have referred. The North still sees the development of the South largely in terms of charity, of how generous we can afford to be politically and economically in times of recession and the loss of living standards. The South, however, sees the issue in radically different terms: as a matter of rights, of the practice of justice which the total situation demands.

Underdevelopment cannot be defined just as economic backwardness; it includes a measure of purposeful injustice. Economic policies have been[16] and are being pursued which act wholly against both the short-term and long-term interests of the approximately one billion destitute of our world.

This issue is covered in much greater depth and with considerably more expertise by Donald Hay in Chapter 3. However, I want to stress here that it should be seen as a human rights issue, with all the moral fervour and indignation that implies, and not just as a matter of technical economic debate. To take one example. Underdeveloped countries depend for day to day solvency on their international credit-worthiness. This in turn depends on their following the economic guidelines of the IMF. This package, euphemistically called 'sound' economic advice, includes measures which have the inevitable effect of sacrificing an improvement in living standards for the poorest of the poor: cut government spending; tighten credit; hold down wages; reduce inflation; remove tariffs which encourage locally-owned industries, in order to attract foreign capital, and remove controls on the remittance of profits overseas.

In terms of long-term economic growth which will really benefit the poor, 'sound' economic advice from the Northern banking community has been proved over and over again to have failed. And yet the same clichés about growth before redistribution are interminably trotted out. Also, it is not sufficiently appreciated that the loss of normal civil liberties in Third World Countries often occur in direct proportion to the kind of economic package which is being implemented. The policy of oppression is closely linked to an insatiable drive for economic privileges or political power.

Now, in the light of the specifically Christian insights into how human nature operates, I believe we can no longer deceive ourselves into believing that the present world economic order is simply the outcome of mistaken economic ideas or cultural differences. It is the result of a deliberate policy which pursues and defends the interests of those who believe that the right to the accumulation and personal enjoyment of wealth is absolute and inalienable.

I have no doubt at all that if instead of me one of the prophets of Israel were writing this chapter, he would say something like the following:-

economic privileges to possess
political power to oppress

15

'Hear, oh countries of the western world, this word of the Lord: you sell the righteous for silver and the needy for a pair of shoes (marked 'made in Brazil'). You trample the heads of the poor into the dust of the earth and turn aside the way of the afflicted. You take exactions from the poor (copper from Chile and Zambia, tin from Bolivia, coffee from Uganda, tea from Sri Lanka, fish from Peru). You have built houses of hewn stone (and filled them with trivial luxuries). Therefore it shall be night to you without vision; the seers (economic advisers) shall be disgraced and the diviners (those who use biblical prophecy to justify the self-interest of their country) shall be put to shame. There is no answer from God.'

What Christians can do to encourage the observance of Human Rights

Fourthly and finally, what can Christians do to encourage the observance of human rights? Denunciation of their abuse, especially when uttered from a remote position of non-involvement, is an easy pastime. It can readily provide a certain moral satisfaction by assuaging the guilt that we might feel. If we are Christians, our calling does not end there. Sheila Cassidy, for example, preaching at the Human Rights Day service in 1980, said:

Too often the role of the Christian in today's world is that of the by-stander. Christ's reaction to the by-standers at his passion was 'terrifying'. He said,

'Weep not for me, weep rather for yourselves and for your children. Rather than weeping for the victims of torture, we should weep for ourselves as guilty by-standers'.[18]

Let me suggest briefly some steps we can take to be involved, so that the implementation of human rights may have a greater chance of success than at present.

i. *Let us work at relating the issues to the Gospel.* This is a negative as well as a positive task, in that we easily confuse the consensus of our particular social group with God's requirement for our lives. Commitment to a particular political party (including the s.d.p.) through good times and bad may easily blind us to underlying biblical principles concerning political activity which need to be clarified and applied. More often than not I tremble when I hear Christians pronounce on political and economic issues, not because of their lack of expertise in these fields, but because they clearly are not thinking from a distinctively Gospel perspective.

Without being able to develop all the implications in detail I would highlight the following points:

(a) Concern for human rights touches all human beings, because their dignity as God's creatures is totally inviolable. For this reason torture comes at the top of the list of abuses, which under no circumstances can have any possible justification.

There are also many less dramatic ways of degrading and coercing human beings. Every human being has the right to be free from being treated as a mere object, a thing, a useful tool to be manipulated.

(b) The touchstone of love after the pattern of Christ is how we respond to those we identify as enemies. In a Gospel perspective even enemies can claim a right to be loved. Thus the means we use to struggle for human rights and social justice are as important as the goals.

(c) The current appeal by many Christians to the notion of 'law and order' has little to do with the Gospel. For law to be an effective instrument in the promotion of a righteous society several conditions must be fulfilled. The law must be based on God's law; it must be administered impartially, justly and mercifully; every citizen must be equally subject to the process of law; and the majority of a nation should be able to see that it has been carried out.

However, in the so-called 'law and order' (or 'National Security') states few, if any, of these conditions are observed. Laws infringing human rights are passed. They depend upon the will and interests of those who wield power. Corruption, murder, unprovoked violence, massive financial swindles often go unpunished when they are committed by people with connections to the ruling authorities.

If God's law is supreme, and if loyalty to Jesus Christ is of the essence of Christian commitment, then in some circumstances laws may well have to be disobeyed in order to uphold the rule of law.

And we dare not use Roman 13 ('Let every person be subject to the governing authorities') as an excuse for total servility to the state. Never has a text of Scripture been so misused in the interests of maintaining an illusion of stability in a society. Those who interpret it to mean unquestioning submission to all the State demands are bound to be quite inconsistent. To take one example: I could guarantee that not one of them, when the crunch came, would be prepared to obey the authorities (on the basis of the Romans passage) if they said, 'you may not give your children Christian instruction', 'you may not assemble together to worship God', 'you may not proclaim Jesus to others'.

And, of course, such total subjection was never intended by Paul. If read properly within its context, and in the light of the rest of Scripture, he was not counselling total, unquestioning obedience, but warning against an easy disobedience. To resist unjust laws and political and economic structures which trample on human rights is one thing; to pretend that we have the right to overthrow any existing order by force in order to bring in the kingdom of God is quite another. In the first case we respond faithfully to God's prophetic word, in the second we are seeking to play at being God, for both vengeance and a new creation are his work, not ours.

Let us, then, pronounce a moratorium on the use of Roman 13 as a basis for saying and doing nothing in a situation of deteriorated human rights.

ii. Let us seek to inform ourselves concerning the real

situations in which human beings are suffering the abuse of their legitimate rights.

In Britain we have relatively little excuse for not discovering what is going on. The International Headquarters of Amnesty International is in London. There are many other bodies engaged in monitoring the implementation, or otherwise, of human rights, not least Church bodies. Of course, in some instances the facts of the case may be distorted, exaggerated or presented in an unbalanced way, in order to achieve maximum ideological and political advantage. It is, therefore, advisable to bear in mind both the ideological stand-point and the ultimate intention of the group which disseminates the information. But never let either of these factors be a justification for indifference. Remember, a rationale for the continuing use of power works at both ends of the ideological spectrum and tends to be both subtle and self-deluding. The fable about the fox and the hedgehog is relevant.[19]

Let us, then, ask the fundamental question, 'In whose interests is the information being put out?' 'Is the manner of its presentation really going to help the afflicted?' We dare not use the rights of real human beings to score political debating points or diplomatic triumphs. For Christians the struggle against human rights violations is an absolute good in itself. There is no higher or long-term good to which it may be sacrificed.

iii. Let us not be afraid of co-operating with any group genuinely concerned to improve the situation of human rights.

Again, this principle of action has a negative as well as a positive aspect. There are some Christians (evangelical believers are often the most guilty offenders) who withdraw fellowship from their brethren because they are willing to co-operate with non-Christian organisations in potesting against injustices.

I suggest that we should be careful not to bring this kind of pressure to bear upon individuals and Churches, and that we should be much more respectful of the motives of others.

The basis on which Christians co-operate in humanitarian service with non-Christians is that of our common humanity and the command to love our neighbours as ourselves. It is also the basis on which God holds all accountable. All people are capable of love, even if they do not acknowledge its divine source. The struggle for human rights is evidence of this love. We should co-operate with our eyes open, not allowing ourselves to be manipulated for the political or ideological ends of others. And we should co-operate whenever and wherever it will be more effective to do so.

The Christian Church world wide has in the recent past a reasonably good record in the fight against human rights violations, though sadly there are some notable exceptions. Sometimes it has been the only body able or willing to confront repressive totalitarian governments. One of its great advantages is its international nature. There are only a few places in the world where Christians are not present. Another advantage is its closeness to ordinary people. There is hardly a Christian family in Argentina, for example, who does not have one of its members, or a friend, or a relative of a friend, on the list of disappeared people. It was this reality which brought home the human rights issue to otherwise indifferent Churches in that country.

Co-operation means active involvement with both governmental and non-governmental bodies. The question of human rights in relation to national diplomatic activity has become a particular issue since the Carter administration used it as a fundamental criterion of foreign policy.

The Fraser-Harkin amendment to the US Foreign Assistance Act (1974–6) cut off first military and then economic aid to countries in which there was evidence of 'a consistent pattern of gross violations of internationally recognised human rights'. The Harkin-Badillo amendment of the International Development Institution Act of 1977 required US representatives of all international financial institutions (with the notable exception of the IMF) to vote against loans to repressive governments, except where aid directly benefits 'needy people.'[20]

Strong arguments are used against the involvement of one government in the human rights affairs of another territory. Evan Luard, former Junior Minister in the British Labour government with responsibility for human rights questions, sets them out in a United Nations Association booklet. [21]

One country's dealings with another are designed to gain the maximum benefit in terms of trade arrangements, cultural exchanges and possible support in world forums for tricky diplomatic negotiating, like that needed for the Middle East or Namibia. Moreover, the country concerned has to protect the lives and interests of its citizens living abroad. A further factor to throw into the balance is the possible strategic value of the country concerned for its geographical location (as South Africa) or its natural resources (as Saudi Arabia). With concerns like these to consider, raising the issue of human rights may not seem to be in a country's long-term interests. In the case of the UK we resent other countries meddling in the affairs of, say, Northern Ireland. Finally, it is argued that intervention is ineffectual anyway; that it may even have the opposite effect, as governments both show their independence and lobby for internal support on grounds of national pride. The present Reagan administration maintains that secret representation is more effective eventually than a kind of 'bull-in-a-china-shop' approach.

However, these arguments are not as substantial as they may appear, as Evan Luard also goes on to show. Few countries attacked on human rights grounds, have themselves broken off diplomatic relations. Britain withdrew its ambassador to Santiago because Chile systematically, widely and brutally flouted the rights of thousands of its citizens.

As a matter of fact, most countries are involved in some way in criticising the internal policies of others. 'It is almost universally recognised that serious violations of human rights are a matter of concern to the International

Community.'[22] The argument against involvement on strategic grounds cuts both ways. The country which criticises may also be of strategic importance in terms of the aid, credit and technological expertise it possesses. Thus the Soviet Union is vulnerable because of its need to import grain, South Africa because of the amount of western investment tied up there. As to whether the campaigns may be effective, let me just say that whatever the motives may have been, President Carter's initial crusade certainly breathed new life and hope into beleagured human rights activists in many Latin American countries, and helped to give some substance to the Human Rights Committee of the Organisation of American States.

Nevertheless, governments are reluctant to get too involved unless the public (you and I) maintain consistent pressure upon them to do so. This can be seen by the present British government's extreme caution over the massive and horrific destruction of human life taking place in El Salvador and Guatemala.

There is much work still to be done. The most pressing need is for the drafting of a satisfactory convention which totally outlaws torture, in any form and under any circumstances, and establishes rules which will govern the rights of mental patients and of those held under suspicion for breaking the law.

International and national mechanisms for promoting and protecting rights also need to be improved.

A United Nations High Commission of Human Rights has been suggested as one possibility. In a world where the systematic slaughter of between 2-3 million people took place only three years ago in Kampuchea, with almost nothing being said or done, there is little room for complacency.[23]

iv. *A Christian is called to suffer.* Grounds for optimism that human rights will improve are not very great. In spite of strenuous representations and masses of publicity, many governments (over one hundred) are abusing their power by depriving citizens of the right to life, health, physical integrity and freedom from harrassment.[24]

In the western world, the right to life of an unborn child and even a severely handicapped child is much attacked and severely compromised. Even Christians are greatly confused. Some, who invoke the biblical testimony concerning God's defense of the weak and the poor to strive for economic policies which will bring them a dignified existence, nevertheless hesitate to press resolutely either the case against abortion on demand or the case for the right of handicapped babies to receive all medical attention necessary for their life to continue. It seems to me there is a great inconsistency here. Can there be a human life more helpless and more unprotected than that of a fetus or a baby?

Arguments used against protecting the life of chronically handicapped babies could be used one day for the humane killing of desperately undernourished children. For what is totally unthinkable to one generation can become imaginable to another, justified by the next and implemented by the following one.

Consistent outspoken opposition to all forms of domination, manipulation, rationalisation and violation will surely be a costly process. We will be tempted to follow prudence, to adopt a 'realistic' policy, or to leave it to the experts. But this is not the way of Christ. He spoke the truth; he practised truth; he engaged in conflict; he experienced opposition; he was abandoned by his friends; and eventually he suffered savage physical violence. There may well be occasions when the willingness to suffer is the only way in which a particularly repressive situation can be unblocked. I know it is easy to affirm this from a safe distance, but I believe South Africa is a case in point. The writing is on the wall. Some would say it has already been there a long time. The hope of radical, lasting, political change through argument and persuasion has dwindled almost to zero. The only alternative seems to be an escalation of violent confrontation between white and black people. Some of the white middle-class Churches, by supporting apartheid, have lost credibility. Can it be that there is any other way of following Christ in South Africa today than by systematic, non-violent non-co-operation with a government which continues to operate laws which are an abomination to God? With the willing-ness of some English-speaking Churches to disobey the 'Immorality Act' by marrying people of different racial backgrounds a beginning has been made.

And, if we are not persuaded that there is a biblical case to be made out for saying no to Caesar and bearing the consequences, then let us remember the ending of the slave trade and of the exploitation of children in factories, the reform of prisons and the founding of labour unions. All these were controversial activities at the time, but Bible-believing Christians were fully involved in their implementation.

Who is sufficient for these things? I believe there is a specific Christian spirituality of resistance to every type of inhumanity. One would need another chapter to develop it. It would certainly include the need to examine deeply one's own life to discover whether there are any roots of oppression still latent there; repentance for a superficial spiritual triumphalism that does not really care about the suffering of a wider world; grace to love those who are brutal, whilst detesting their brutality; grace to under-stand those who disagree with our opinions and falsely call into question our motives; persevering prayer for the work of the Holy Spirit to restrain and bind the satanic in people and to release them from its power; courage to proclaim the good news of Christ, which alone can free people from the fear and greed that often cause inhuman actions and policy; and solidarity with our brethren who are already suffering much for the sake of Christ.

Such a spirituality, which would include other ingre-dients as well, would be applicable to all the topics under review in this book. 'A spirituality for the year 2000 AD'; Yes, we need it very urgently, before it is too late.

1 Cf. the case of Petr Uhl, *Prisoners of Conscience* (Amnesty International, London, 1981), pp. 7-8.
2 Cf. 'Declaration and Letters' from the Roumanian Christian Committee for the Defence of Religious Freedom and Conscience, signed 1 and 5 July, 1978.
3 Morning Star, 27th July 1978.
4 E.g. the case of Denis Cousin. He was detained for 60 days under *arrêts de rigueur* in France for refusal to do military service. He was, however, released with the change of government in May, 1981. *Prisoners of Conscience*, op cit. p. 34.
5 Examples are in the distinction made between 'patrial' and 'non patrial' descendants; the case of *ius soli* – the right of people born in the United Kingdom to be full British Citizens, and the lack of right to appeal against refusal of naturalisation or registration.
6 Cf. *The Repression Trade* (Amnesty International, London, 1981).
7 In these two cases it has been pointed out that the right to life is not in the authority of the state to confer through legislative decision. It is an absolute right which the state has an obligation to administer on behalf of all its citizens.
8 Confining the present selection of cases of human rights violations to the western world has been deliberate. It is too easy to believe that the problem exists only in totalitarian states on the other side of the world. Later on in this study other – more infamous – situations will also be discussed.
9 Cf. David M. Paton (ed.), *Breaking Barriers: Nairobi 1975*. (S.P.C.K., London, 1976), pp. 169-172.
10 On the very same day in July 1980 that it became known that a British citizen, Claire Wilson, had been tortured by the Chilean secret police, the British Government announced a resumption of arms sales, including security equipment, to the Chilean armed forces. Cf. *The Repression Trade*, op. cit. p. iv. Strong protests by the British Council of Churches, Cardinal Hume, Amnesty International, members of various political parties and others went unheeded.
11 *Thirty Years of Human Rights*. (London. 1980), p.7.
12 Our attitude to different economic systems will be determined by the weight we give to a variety of biblical principles. Those, for example, who take the practice of usury to be an absolute moral injustice, prohibited for all time by God's law, will consider this a very powerful argument for

the ending of the Capitalist economy and replacing it with a socialist one where, theoretically, profits are distributed to everyone equally, and not to some individuals at the expense of others.

13 'The Christian Basis of Concern for Human Rights', BCC Consultation (3rd December 1980).
14 Possessing a strong theoretical base for affirming the meaning of human rights does not mean that, in practice, we have any right to impose our views by undue coercion. The means we use to put over our opinions must accord with the Spirit of Christ – prayer, persuasion, lobbying, and so on. If a country either denies or accords rights which seem to us to constitute a very fundamental denial of God's view of human and right, then we are left the recourse of refusing to accept the state's decision. This is the case of conscientous objection. We must seek first to use every available channel the present laws allow us to try to change them. Then our opposition should, I believe, only take the form of non-violent protest.
15 *Human Rights: a Study in Biblical Themes* (Grove Books, Bramcote, 1979), pp. 12, 16.
16 Cf. Walter Rodney, *How Europe Underdeveloped Africa*. C. T. Kurien, *Poverty and Development* (Madras. 1974).
17 op. cit. p. 7
18 'No to torture'. Human Rights Day Service. 1980.
19 One day a fox came across a hedgehog in his path. The hedgehog immediately rolled into a tight prickly ball. The fox said to him:
   'Oh, Mr Hedgehog, if you would remove your prickles you and I could be friends.'
   To which the hedgehog replied:
   'Oh no, Mr Fox, we could only be friends if you were to remove your teeth as well!'
20 Cf. 'The Links between Human Rights and Basic Needs.' *Background*. Centre for International Policy. Spring, 1978.
21 *Human Rights and Foreign Policy*. (Pergamon Press, Oxford) 1981.
22 Ibid, p. 8
23 Other cases of genocide have been documented by Leo Kuper, *Genocide*. (Penguin 1981).
24 Cf. *The Repression Trade*, o.c.

2 The Arms Race: the Defence Debate

Rather than expect one lecturer to handle the range of Christian attitudes to war in the nuclear age, the London Lectures Committee invited Dr Alan Kreider to present one viewpoint and Lord Cameron another.

A. Nuclear Weaponry and Pacifism

Dr Alan Kreider
(*Director of the London Mennonite Centre*)

'The present insanity of the global arms race, if continued, will lead inevitably to a conflagration so great that Auschwitz will seem like a minor rehearsal.' These are the words, not of Michael Foot or E. P. Thompson, but of Dr Billy Graham, speaking – deeply moved – in 1978 at the site of the Auschwitz concentration camp. Dr Graham has not always thought like this. But now he is speaking out against the arms race and urging other Christians to do likewise. His 'change of heart' is rooted in his realisation of the enormity of the consequences of this issue. Unless it is dealt with creatively and Christianly, it will very likely render irrelevant all the other topics in this book. If the world does not get this issue right, we shall not reach the year 2000 AD.

It is hard to come to terms imaginatively with the abyss into which we are peering. But statistics are of some help to us.

The two super-powers not only have between them over 15,000 strategic nuclear warheads. Scattered through their arsenals they also have an astonishing array of tactical nuclear weapons, including nuclear depth bombs, nuclear artillery shells and nuclear torpedos, totalling approximately 27,000 warheads. When the weapons of the second-rank nuclear powers are added, we reach a world total of approximately 50,000 warheads. The estimated destructive capacity of these bombs is 15,000,000 kilotons, one million times the explosive force of the bomb which devastated Hiroshima.[2]

The effects of even a small proportion of these weapons would be awesome, if they were to be used. In a dispassionate study, the US Congress Office of Technology Assessment has estimated that in a one-megaton American attack on one Russian city, Leningrad, 890,000 people would die 'promptly' (within thirty days), and most of the estimated 1,260,000 injured would also die prematurely. In a Soviet counter-force attack on American military bases, between 2 and 22 million people could be expected to die 'promptly'. And in an allout attack, between 35 and 77 per cent of the American people would be 'prompt' fatalities.[3] As for the United Kingdom, a recent authoritative study has concluded:

> 'Britain is one of the most densely populated countries in the world. It also has one of the highest concentrations of nuclear weapons bases . . . Britain is likely to fare badly under a large nuclear attack, with perhaps no more than a few million people surviving the first month.'[4]

Doubts about Deterrence

But there are other ways that are more helpful than statistics in becoming conscious of the catastrophe which looms over us. Billy Graham did so poetically and prophetically by evoking the image of Auschwitz and the holocaust. Lord Mountbatten in one of his last speeches did so

28

more personally by asking his audience to listen with him to the terrifying testimony of a survivor of Hiroshima:

> Suddenly a glaring whitish, pinkish light appeared in the sky accompanied by an unnatural tremor which was followed almost immediately by a wave of suffocating heat and a wind which swept away everything in its path. Within a few seconds the thousands of people in the streets in the centre of the town were scorched by a wave of searing heat. Many were killed instantly, others lay writhing on the ground screaming in agony from the intolerable pain of their burns. Everything standing upright in the way of the blast – walls, houses, factories and other buildings – was annihilated . . . Hiroshima had ceased to exist.[5]

However we conceptualise it, nuclear war would be, in the laconic words of the Office of Technology Assessment, 'a calamity unprecedented in human history.'[6]

Deterrence may, of course, be averting the calamity, at least temporarily. Official voices repeatedly reassure us that 'deterrence is working today as it has worked for the past thirty-six years.'[7] There may be some truth in these comfortable words. But there are also disquieting indications that our massive power is not giving us any great sense of security. Public discussion of the world military situation is fearful and is dominated by the word 'threat'. 'In the arms race of the last decade', we were told in 1981 by a government minister, 'there has been only one runner, the Soviet Union.'[8] Mrs Thatcher has often returned to this theme: '(The Russians') military strength is growing. (They) do not publish their intentions. So we must judge them by their military capabilities.'[9] In the light of the 'Soviet threat', Sir Neil Cameron has argued, the British government must arouse 'the full support of the nation' for further military expenditure by convincing the nation that 'the threat is real and with us now. We must get this across.'[10]

The threat is certainly real. The Warsaw Pact forces are formidable. They have almost five million men under arms. But we should not underestimate the threat which we ourselves pose. NATO also has almost five million soldiers. And facing the Russians to the East, on their dreaded second front, is China, with almost five million troops.[11] The Russians are certainly also aware of the unreliability of many of the forces of their Eastern European allies.[12] Measured by weapons, the situation is similar. The Warsaw Pact has a 1.5 to 1 advantage over NATO in tanks; but NATO has a 4 to 1 advantage over the Warsaw Pact in anti-tank guided weapons.[13] In strategic nuclear weapons, the USSR leads the US in throw-weight and total megatonnage; but in total warheads and the crucial area of accuracy the US is ahead (see Table 1). [14] It is the Soviets who, in view of US capabilities, have greater cause to feel vulnerable to a first strike. Nevertheless the US is proceeding to deploy the precisely targetable Trident D5 and will shortly be constructing the super-accurate M-X missile system.

Table 1.

Strategic Weapons of Superpowers (1980)

	Number of Delivery Vehicles	Throw-weight	Megatonnage (approx.)	Number of Warheads	Accuracy of Advanced Re-entry Vehicle
	(no.)	(millions of lbs.)	(mt.)	(no.)	(CEP: metres)
USSR	2,504	11.3	4,800	6,000	500 (SS-18)
USA	2,064	7.2	3,200	9,200	200 (Mk. 12-A)
Total	4,568	18.5	8,000	15,200	

Source: *SIPRI Yearbook 1980*, xxvii–xxix, 222.

Even in theatre nuclear weapons the Soviet position is not preponderant (see Table 2). Their SS-20 missile, which is the justification for NATO's forthcoming deployment of Cruise and Pershing II missiles, is a major new

Table 2

Theatre Nuclear Weapons: Europe

	NATO	Warsaw Pact
Short-range (under 100 mi.): est.	7,000	3,500
Medium-range		
Missile warheads*	742	1,335
Aircraft-delivered warheads	1,170	3,095
Total	9,912	7,930

*includes 400 Poseidon warheads assigned to NATO.
Sources: *The Military Balance, 1981–1982* (IISS), 128–129; M. Leitenberg, 'Background Information', in F. Barnaby, ed., *Tactical Nuclear Weapons* (SIPRI, 1978), pp. 17, 78.

weapons system. At the moment they have a theoretical availability of 410 warheads for use in Western Europe.[15] But for years the US has assigned to NATO 'a submarine-based nuclear force of immense destructive power' – 400 Poseidon warheads[16] – and, in short-range theatre weapons, NATO has a 2 to 1 superiority.[17] Furthermore, although the Soviet theatre weapons cannot reach America, NATO's theatre weapons can strike at the Russian heartland.[18]

So the Warsaw Pact is fearsomely strong; so also is NATO. Nevertheless both alliances feel threatened. This is not only because of ministerial exaggeration, swollen expenditures, and the sheer immensity of the forces being arrayed by both sides. It is also because, as a result of the arms race, deterrence is fraying badly and is in danger of splitting wide open at the seams.[19] Deterrence, of couse, has never delivered what many of its more grandiose proponents have claimed. It has not given the *world* thirty-five years of *peace* in any convincing sense of these words. At best, it has given *Europe* thirty-five years of more and more heavily armed cold war; in the Third World, it has by no means prevented numerous savage wars resulting in today's sixteen million refugees.[20] Indeed, it is arguable that deterrence has facilitated these wars precisely because nuclear-armed great powers are, for fear of each other, less free to play a constructive role, individually or jointly, in Third World disputes.

Even in Europe, where the bombs have not fallen yet, the future of deterrence is bleak, overshadowed by two interrelated forces. First, there is the march of technology, which some consider to be an autonomous cause of the arms race.[21] Technology has succeeded, for example, in miniaturising nuclear weapons, whose small size has enabled them to be disseminated throughout all branches of the armed forces and whose relatively low yield has diminished the 'firebreak' between conventional and nuclear weapons, thereby offering a much more plausible possibility of use than do their strategic counterparts. And if, as is NATO's declared intention under the strategy of 'flexible response', we actually made first use of the battlefield weapons which the burgeoning technology has offered us, the result would probably be total nuclear war. Lord Mountbatten asserted, 'I cannot imagine a situation in which nuclear weapons would be used as battle field weapons without the conflagration spreading.'[22] *The Military Balance, 1981-1982*, just published by the International Institute of Strategic Studies, agrees.[23]

A 'flexible response' would quickly become inflexible, to the detriment of us all.

Technology has also refined the guidance systems of nuclear delivery vechicles, enabling remarkable precision. A Trident D5 missile will be capable of being fired by a submerged submarine, of flying 6,000 nautical miles, and of delivering eight or more 75 kiloton warheads, each to within tens of metres of individual targets at considerable distance of each other.[24] Thus, the second influence undermining deterrence – a change in strategic doctrine from MAD ('Mutually Assured Destruction') to 'counterforce' – is made necessary by this phenomenal accuracy. For three decades deterrence theory had been based upon the doctrine of MAD entailing threats to destroy entire cities ('counter-value' or 'counter-city targeting'). But the new generation of precise nuclear weapons has required the development of a new strategic doctrine known as 'counter-force' targeting.[25] This theory, implemented in President Carter's Presidential Directive 59, calls for the capacity to threaten a 'prolonged but limited' nuclear war by attacking missile silos, command centres and airbases (with nevertheless inevitable collateral deaths of millions of civilians through fallout). This doctrine has led both to the contemplation of a nuclear 'first-strike' against the Russians and to the alarming realisation that the Russians may be planning the same thing, with the concomitant and highly dangerous need to threaten to 'launch on warning' (i.e., to launch missiles from silos as soon as available information makes it apparent that the other side may have launched an attack against those silos). As a result, the strategic forces of both alliances are increasingly on edge. The notorious American false-alarms of 1979-80 were signs of this jumpiness, and raise the sobering possibility that some future computer malfunction could initiate a series of escalating responses by both powers that could quickly become uncontrollable.[26]

The authorities, of course, assure us that their fail-safe devices are infallible. Even if this were so, it is unlikely to be the case in Third World countries, where – thanks to widespread civil nuclear technology – the proliferation of nuclear weapons within the next few years is all too probable. By the mid-1980s, according to an adviser to US Defense Secretary Caspar Weinberger, as many as thirty-five countries will have been able to extract from their 'civilian' reactors enough plutonium to construct 'several dozen' nuclear bombs.[27] The political volatility of many of these regimes requires no comment, and the risk of a nuclear war between them before the end of the 1980s must be regarded as very considerable. The probability of the superpowers becoming involved in such a war must also appear to be high. No wonder we feel insecure and threatened. It is for good reason that the Doomsday Clock

33

of the *Bulletin of the Atomic Scientists* is poised at four minutes to midnight.

Nevertheless, rejecting alternatives, we persevere, each year committing ourselves more irrevocably to the policies that are shackling us. The escalating costs of this policy should in themselves be sobering. They have now reached levels which our forefathers would have found incredible. Had we not been conditioned by the gradual character of the increase to tolerate such peacetime expenditures, we also would be shocked by them. In 1980 the world spent $550,000 million (£312,000 million) on armaments.[28] This represents 6 per cent of total world output, in real terms twice the percentage being spent during the great arms race preceding World War I and during the 'missile gap' of 1960.[29] At best, the preemption of resources for defence purposes cannot be represented as more than a second-best use of those resources. No less an authority than Dwight Eisenhower characterised the resulting diversion of resources from the poor as 'theft'.[30] Thus we continue to build new missile systems. We export new weapons to our Third World friends of the moment, hoping that they will not be fired at our own ships or fall into the Russians' hands through defeat or a coup. And our Russian adversaries, sensing themselves beleaguered and boxed in, are no more creative than we are.

The result is a race, a race in which we are running faster and faster to remain in the same place, a race that has no finishing line. To my mind, we are less threatened by the Russians than we are by the arms race itself. How will it end? It is not polite to ask; but this is the central question that the proponents of deterrence must answer. Are we to live well down into the Twenty-First Century or longer – if the Lord delays his return – with our security depending upon the continued development and deployment, by an increasing number of countries, of such dangerous weapons? Privately, despite their confident public assertions, many of the proponents of deterrence confess their fears of the inevitabilty of nuclear war. For although they

34

differ about the size and immediacy of the risk that nuclear weapons will be used, they know that 'a small risk endured for a sufficiently long time brings the certainty that the risk will be fulfilled.'[31] Moreover, the prudence of running even a small risk should be crucially determined by the scale of the consequences, should the contingency arise: a company, for example, with guarantees measured in £000s, dares not risk investing £ millions even if there is only a small chance that this investment will fail. The 1981 Defence White Paper states, 'The first obligation of any government is the defence of the realm.'[32] By its own criterion, a criterion of what will work, the UK government's policies to that end must at best be regarded as a very considerable gamble.

Biblical Considerations

But as Christians we can never stop with analysing the effectiveness of a policy. We must also assess its faithfulness to God's will as revealed in Scripture. And by this standard as well, the policies undergirding the arms race are misguided. Not only are they not working; they are wrong.

Throughout the Old Testament, God revealed that his nature, as well as his ultimate goal for humanity, is peace, *shalom*, an all-embracing wholeness and justice. Nevertheless war, along with famine and pestilence, was something that he brought about for judgment. Early in the history of Israel God is recorded as fighting on behalf of his people against their pagan foes.[33] Often he won their battles for them by miracle – by a crumbling wall, hornets, thunder, a loud sound. God wanted it to be clear that his victories were gifts of his grace, not the result of human works (e.g., Judg. 7:2-3).

To ensure that his people would trust in him and not in their own strength, God established certain rules. In Deuteronomy 20:1-9 he specified that their armies were to be numerically inferior to their foes; in Joshua 11:6 he commanded that they be technologically inferior as well –

they were not to have chariots, and were to burn any chariots that they captured. There was good reason for this. Chariots were the capital weapons of the ancient world. There was something seductive about their speed and destructiveness which led people to trust in them. And since people worship what they put their ultimate reliance in (e.g., Psalm 115:3-11), God's people would be committing idolatry – committing rebellion against himself – if they adopted chariots.

By choosing to have a human king who would 'go before us and fight our battles', the Israelites rejected God as their kingly defender and began the process of accommodation to the patterns of life of surrouding societies (1 Sam. 8). Soon, as Samuel had predicted, they were developing a professional army, entering into alliances, and building chariots. Thereafter, through his prophets, God denounced his idolatrous people. 'Woe to those who go down to Egypt for help and rely on horses, and trust in chariots because they are many and in horsemen because they are strong, and do not look to the Holy One of Israel . . .' (Isa. 31.1). God, who had fought for his people, now fought against them. 'Behold, I am against you . . . and I will burn your chariots in smoke' (Nahum 2:13). Often he used for this purpose the pagan nations themselves – terrifying, idolatrous, totalitarian societies – which were his instruments of judgment quite as much as Israel had been earlier. A major cause of his people's plight was their militaristic infidelity. 'Because you have trusted in chariots and in the multitude of your warriors, therefore the tumult of war shall arise . . . and all your fortresses shall be destroyed' (Hosea 10:13-14). The implications of the Old Testament for the ethics of war are staggering, and are very different from what Christians have often inferred.

In the New Testament, in his Son Jesus, the promised Messiah, God fulfilled the Old Testament. Christians have had two ways of understanding the implictions of this fulfilment for warfare. One of these is Pacifism/

Nonviolence.[34] Pacifists emphasize that although in the Old Testament God's people fought, there was also an anticipation of a fuller realisation of God's intentions, of a new order, to be ushered in by the Messiah. Zechariah (9:9-10) prophesied that the coming King would not only come humbly on a donkey; he would also 'cut off the chariot' from Israel and 'command peace to the nations'. And when Jesus came, he did precisely that. In a violent situation in which expectant Jews were advocating a righteous war against the exploitative occupying Romans, Jesus came with something creative, with a message whose newness scandalised his hearers. 'Love your enemies!'[35] In Luke (6:27) that is Jesus' very first ethical pronouncement. Love the Romans, love your atheist oppressors, love those whom you are tempted to resist by collective violence. Love them because God loves them; he loves the unjust as well as the just. And in loving them you will be entering into the character of your Father. Children of God imitate their Father. And, says Jesus in Matthew (5:9, 45), it is peacemakers and enemy-lovers who are God's children. Such people do not need to fear, for the Father has chosen to give them the kingdom (Luke 12:32); he has loved them, his former enemies (Rom. 5:10). Through his grace they have been converted, turned around. They have been reborn into a new family which is living by new values, the teachings of the Messiah.

This message threatened the Roman/Jewish establishment so much that it did away with the troublemaker by crucifixion. But God vindicated the foolishness of his Messiah by miracle, by resurrection; the new order was a gift of grace, not of works. God then empowered the church with a sword, the sword of the Spirit. And for three centuries the members of this 'Christian counter-culture' challenged the Roman empire.[36] Emphasising enemy-love, they refused to take life, even in time of war. And although (in obedience to Romans 13:1-7) they emphasised subordination to the state, they were willing, in response to a higher loyalty, when necessary, nonviolently to resist the state. Despite persecution, they grew. Throughout the history of the church their pacifism has lived on – in the lives of prophetic witnesses such as St Francis, Peter Chelcicky, George Fox, André Trocmé and Martin Luther King, in renewal groups, within a counter-culture.[37] It is this position which I personally hold.

In the Christian culture which was established after Constantine, a new position came to the fore. This was the just war theory, which for 1,600 years had been the official position of the major Christian traditions, including the Church of England.[38] Adherents of the just war theory are sensitive throughout the Bible to God's concern for the innocent. 'Far be it from you', Abraham argued with God, 'to slay the righteous with the wicked . . . Shall not the Judge of all the earth do right?' (Gen. 18:25). God enshrined the criterion of justice in the Law. 'Do not slay the innocent and righteous, for I will not acquit the wicked' (Exo. 23:7). And there is, just war theorists believe, a sameness of substance between the testaments. John the Baptist, far from telling the soldiers to leave the forces, established rules for the just conduct of their profession. Just war theorists are also convinced that Paul, in Romans 13:4-5, by stating that the government bears the sword to execute judgment on the wrongdoer, has established the criterion of justice in the use of force.

In order to translate these principles into political reality, Augustine and later thinkers in the just war tradition established some criteria.[39] A war would be just if, and only if, three conditions were met. There must be a right intention; soldiers, even in the thick of the fight, must 'cherish the spirit of a peacemaker'. In the second place, there must be a just cause; war is only just if it is a response to a manifest violation of justice. And, in the third place, there must be just means. The means must be proportionate – not wreaking more havoc than was warranted by the original injury. The means must also be discriminate – soldiers will be just only if they restrict their killing to other combatants, not to civilians, women and children. There is therefore a difference, Just War theorists have maintained, between war and massacre. For example, a war which begins in response to a just cause, if waged in an unjust manner, ceases to be a just war, and killing in it becomes murder. And if the war is not just, the Christian must refuse involvement, if necessary by disobeying and taking the consequences.

Both pacifism and the just war theory have fallible histories.[40] Pacifists have been self-righteous and irresponsible. They have tended to withdraw from conflict rather than seeking alternative solutions by nonviolent means. Just War theorists have also been unfaithful. They have too easily assumed that their side's cause was just. They have colluded in unjust means, such as the allied obliteration bombing of German cities during the Second World War. Nevertheless, pacifism and the just war theory stand as the two Christian traditions of thinking about warfare. Both, like all ethical systems worthy of respect, establish boundaries. Even if theatened by a totalitarian, God-denying enemy who brandishes immoral weapons, they affirm that there are moral limits beyond which we Christians dare not go in combating that immorality – lest we become like the enemy. By the measure of either teaching, it is clear that just war theorists and pacifists must say 'no' to nuclear weaponry.

It is not that other weapons, according to just war criteria, cannot also be used unjustly. Dresden was as immorally indiscriminate as Hiroshima. Nuclear weapons, however, pose a much more formidable moral problem than the conventional high explosive bomb, for with nuclear weapons discrimination and proportion are much harder to achieve. Because of their tremendous explosive power, because of their radiation and fallout, because of the improbability of arresting escalation, because of the incredible problems of communication, command and control, nuclear weapons are a new phenomenon in the history of warfare. They are intrinsically indiscriminate, and thus intrinsically unjust.[41] Their use leads to massacre, to genocide. Even the threat to use them is immoral. What we think in our hearts, said Jesus (Matt. 5.28), is as important as what we do. And the threat to commit genocide, which must be credible to be effective, is no more moral than genocide itself.[42] In a Remembrance Sunday sermon in 1979 John Stott well summarised the just war case against strategic nuclear weapons. Because they are 'indiscriminate in their effects, destroying combatants and noncombatants alike, it seems clear to me that they are ethically indefensible, and that every Christian, whatever he may think of the possibility of a "just" use of conventional weapons, must be a nuclear pacifist.'[43]

A Common Front

Thus nuclear weapons have brought pacifists and many just war theorists, for the first time in history, into a single movement. In the face of the arms race, these are not opposing positions; they are two ways of coming to the same conclusion. Both total pacifists and nuclear pacifists regard the arms policies of governments East and West as immoral. Both of us recognise that the nuclear weapons which are designed to produce security are in fact producing fear, and thus greater insecurity. Both of us are awed by the momentum of the arms race that we are called to struggle against. Yet both of us are convinced that technology must be governed by morality, and not vice versa. To affirm these convictions deeply and to assert them in public life will require repentance, turning around, possibly at a heavy cost.[44] The consequences of our actions may be suffering. Yet we affirm that God will honour those who trust him enough to take risky steps of obedience. As the three young men in a hopeless situation told King Nebuchadnezzar (Dan. 3:17-18), 'Our God whom we serve is able to deliver us from the burning fiery furnace; and he will deliver us out of your hands, O king. But if not, . . . we (still) will not serve your gods . . .'

But pacifists and adherents of the just war have more in

40

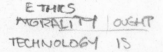
ETHICS
MORALITY | OUGHT
TECHNOLOGY IS

common than a rejection of nuclear weapons and a willingness to suffer. We are united by four affirmations. One of these is that the arms race, although it can cataclysmically supersede the other issues with which this book deals, is in reality intertwined with all of them. We therefore affirm that our military insecurity is not solely a result of the 'Soviet threat' or of military considerations in general. Our insecurity is equally a product of the 'energy crisis', which because of the insatiable appetite of the First World leads to our determination to extract – by Rapid Deployment Forces, if necessary – 'our' oil supplies from the Arab nations. Our insecurity is also a result of the unbridled momentum of technology, which does more to dictate the development of new, strategically destabilising weaponry than does the will of statesmen or even military necessity.[45] Also contributing to our insecurity are economic structures and policies, which are exacerbating the disparity of wealth between North and South, and which, if present trends in development and nuclear proliferation continue, could lead to nuclear blackmail by the poor nations against the rich nations.[46] Racism and the lack of human rights are also sources of our insecurity. There will be turbulence in the strategically vital areas of Southern Africa and the Middle East until black Africans and the Palestinians are given self-determination and equal economic opportunity. Finally, our insecurity is a product of the 'security business' itself, of the 'military-industrial complexes' of East and West, whose unchallengeable power undermines disarmament initiatives and syphons off the first-fruits of our societies' investment and research, thereby leading to social deprivation and unrest.[47] This intertwining of issues is clearly set forth in Scripture. The biblical concept of peace (*shalom*, *eirēnē*) is comprehensive.[48] Only the false prophets thought that peace could be achieved without justice and compassion for the weak. Our current military insecurity is God's indictment of our blinkered assumptions and self-serving policies. We will have no peace until we repent.

Adherents of the Just War and pacifists also make a second affirmation – that Christians must resist the dehumanisation, the demonisation of the enemy. This is not only because Jesus calls us to love our enemy. It is also because there is a darker side to ourselves – and to our allies – which prevents us from throwing the first stone.[49] Furthermore, there are qualities in our enemy which we often overlook. In the Soviet Union, for example, despite severe repression and a regime of militant godlessness, 20 per cent of the populace are actively Christian; in the UK the figure is only 11 per cent.[50] Perhaps the seduction of ease is more asphyxiating of Christian belief than persecution. Immense evil has come about in the past from the assumptions that God is on our side and that the enemy is the 'Antichrist'. As one Jewish scholar put it, speaking out of his own people's bitter experience, 'Dehumanisation is an early warning of holocaust.'[51]

A third affirmation that pacifists and adherents of the just war make together is that Christians are called to seek reconciliation. Enmity, the Christian message proclaims, is not necessarily eternal. In Christ, who is our peace, the dividing wall between hostile social groupings, between Jew and Gentile, has been breached (Eph. 2:13-16); the goal of history in Christ is the reconciliation of the whole universe to himself (Col. 1.20). We now seek events that partake of something of the character of this consummation, and if we stop to reflect, we can recognise them. A significant example is the ending of the centuries-old enmity between Germany and France; both have seen that their welfare exists, not in conflict, but in interdependence. Might this not be equally true of Russia and the West? But, it will be objected, in the words of the 1981 Defence White Paper, the Russians are a threat because of their 'hostile and expansionist' Marxist-Leninist ideology.[52] Yet what is thought-provoking is the fact that western military experts, who in the 1961 Defence White Paper viewed China along with Russia as an enemy, are now viewing her as a collaborator, if not as an actual ally.[53]

What has changed? Not China's ideology, which remains a variant of Marxist-Leninism. What has brought about this partial reconciliation is rather the perception, by both the West and the Chinese, that they face a common enemy – the Soviet Union. When will the West and the Russians perceive that we too face a common enemy – mutual obliteration – and that we must seek reconciliation for the common good?

A fourth affirmation that Christian pacifists and adherents of the war make together is that there *are* alternatives. We may not know fully what these are, but it is a divine calling, in the face of immorality, to search for them. Alternatives will not come into being, however, unless believers wrestle with the Scriptures, pray, and do hard and imaginative thinking. As we do these things we may be called dreamers, and our thinking may be dismissed as half-baked. But it is unreasonable for anyone to expect us to have fully-baked policies, since very little civil-service time and negligible funding have gone into the seach for alternatives. The one organisation that has been doing significant work in this area, the Alternative Defence Commission of the University of Bradford, has an 18-month budget of £26,000; the research and development budget of the Ministry of Defence for 1981 – 1982 is £1.67 thousand million pounds . . . 64,230 times as large![54]

Alternatives to the Nuclear Deterrent

As we search for alternatives to the nuclear arsenal,[55] adherents of the just war theory and pacifists are bound to differ at times. The former will be more comfortable than pacifists with one alternative – a bolstering of manifestly defensive conventional forces.[56] This is also the case with a second alternative – territorial defence in depth on the model of Switzerland or Sweden.[57] On a third alternative, however, they can agree – non-violent civilian defence. Throughout history much of the most effective pressure for social change, and for defence, has been

43

non-violent. Historians have begun to write about this only recently, and the story is a fascinating one.[58] Arguably, in the nuclear age, nonviolent civilian defence is not only more moral than any other defence strategy; it also makes more sense. This was the conclusion of Sir Basil Liddell-Hart, one of the most insightful strategic thinkers of the twentieth century. In his interviews with German generals after World War II, Liddell-Hart found that '*violent* forms of resistance had not been very effective or troublesome to them', for they knew how to cope with these. But they had been baffled and disconcerted by the *nonviolent* resistance which they encountered in Denmark, Holland and Norway. When resistance became violent they were actually relieved! What did this mean, Liddell-Hart pondered, for defence in the nuclear age, in which the prospects of foreseeable defence policies were annihilation? In 1967 he proposed an alternative defence, based on nonviolent resistance. 'It is necessary to demonstrate', he concluded, 'that (nonviolent civilian defence) is a workable policy, and that it is more workable than military defence.'[59] Liddell-Hart was a prophet. According to Sir Neil Cameron, he was 'one who in his time was challenging the nation, and the military, to think about the problems of the future.'[60] Can we respond to his challenge? It would require careful study, national education, and organisation in advance of the crisis. If brought to the test, Christian churches might be at the heart of this – as communities of resistance.[61]

Whichever of these alternative stances we adopt, we must also work for a corresponding shift in UK nuclear weapons policy. This could begin with some unilateral gesture, such as deferring or scrapping plans for the deployment of Trident or Cruise missiles. But in view of the dictates of Christian morality, it must go further, to the rejection by the UK of all nuclear weapons, and the withdrawal of British facilities to American nuclear forces. It could involve the UK staying within NATO as a non-nuclear-weapon state (like Denmark and Canada), or more likely, leaving NATO altogether. There is no single, straight-forward route to a policy of nuclear disarmament.[62]

But adherents of the just war theory and pacifists agree in saying that some unilateral action is necessary. Of course, multilateral disarmament remains the goal, but it cannot be the start of the means. It has been tried already for three decades, and has ended up with so-called 'arms control ' – which is a euphemistic way of describing the biggest arms buildup in history. Unfortunately, multilateralism is unlikely to start spontaneously, for both sides, with good reason, fear each other too much. Some country, in hope, in far-sighted realism, has got to risk breaking that cycle of fear. And there is not much time left.

The United Kingdom, as a small nuclear weapons state, is ideally situated to begin this process. If we did so, we not only would be keeping our side of the 1968 Nonproliferation Treaty, Article VI of which requires nuclear weapons states to limit vertical proliferation – the proliferation of their own weapons; we would also be helping to impede horizontal proliferation, by strengthening the hands of statesmen in non-nuclear weapons states who are struggling to keep Article II, thereby staving off the collapse of their side of the treaty.[63] Indeed, through unilateral disarmament the United Kingdom, which has lost its empire, might discover that it had a new role in the world. As a small nuclear power and a base for a nuclear colossus, we have been straitjacketed in an uncreative posture. Our much-extolled 'seat at the counsels of the mighty' has not produced initiatives for disarmament. Our bomb is too small to influence the great powers towards sanity. We can only really influence them – and many other countries – by getting rid of it.

Of course this is risky. It might alter alliance structures; it might make the Russians more ambitious; it might make the Americans more irresponsible; it might even, as Lord Carrington has reminded us, make nuclear war more likely.[64] We have to weigh these risks. But we must also remember that there are risks in the current British policy. These are massive risks, risks of the nuclear annihilation of both us and our enemies, risks of what must be the ultimate mortal sin. These risks are becoming more real every day. Current policy, as a cursory reading of the daily newspapers makes clear, is failing; a new policy – even a risky one, but more probably a less risky one – is needed. For the sake of a breakthrough in the intractable conflict between Israel and the Arab world, President Anwar Sadat of Egypt put himself in his enemies' hands, thereby risking his reputation and his life. The world desperately needs a statesperson who will act with equal vision and courage in an attempt to end the arms race.

At the end of the day, this is not a matter to be decided by calculating risks; it is a matter of faith, of faithfulness to our God, of trust in his sovereignty and not in our works. There are times when we Christians, because of our obedience to our Lord, regardless of the risks, must say 'No thank you.' We are severe in our judgment of those German Christians whose agnostic complacency in the Nazi era enabled Auschwitz to take place. How will future Christians, indeed how will Almighty God himself judge us if we fail to respond to the challenges of our time?

A century and a half ago a group of Christians set out to abolish one of the inevitabilities of life, slavery. They encountered much opposition. 'Nowhere,' it was argued by their opponents, 'does the Bible condemn slavery; slavery is a beneficial institution; it is economically necessary; it is rooted in human nature; it is backed by the authority of the State to which Christians must submit; if *we* do not trade slaves, the French will; abolitionism is utopianism.'[65] Our Christian forbears were not deterred by these arguments, and so by God's grace a movement came into being, and an inevitability was dethroned. How foolish their detractors look today. What if Christians in our time were to get a vision of peace, and set out to work for it? What if we really believed that God can work miracles, and that inevitabilities are therefore not inevitable? Is God calling some of us to step out in faith in a new abolitionist movement to end the arms race before the year 2000 AD?[66]

The foregoing chapter (with its notes which follow) is substantially the same as the lecture delivered in the debate of 9 November 1981; it has not been altered to accommodate later events or data. Alan Kreider wishes to express his gratitude to the members of the Shaftesbury Project's 'Study Group on War and Peace' for providing encouragement, argument and evidence.

1 Billy Graham, 'A Change of Heart', *Sojourners*, August 1979, pp. 12–14.
2 *World Armaments and Disarmament, SIPRI Yearbook 1980* (London, Taylor & Francis, 1980), pp. xxv–xxix, 222; Robert Neild, *How to Make Up Your Mind about the Bomb* (London, Andre Deutsch, 1981), p. 31.
3 US Congress, Office of Technology Assessment, *The Effects of Nuclear War* (Washington, DC, Government Printing Office, 1979), pp. 37, 140 (UK edition, London, Croom Helm, 1980).
4 Peter Goodwin, *Nuclear War: The Facts on our Survival* (London, Ash & Grant, 1981), p. 114.
5 Earl Mountbatten, 'The Final Abyss?', speech given on the occasion of the award of the Louise Weiss Foundation Prize to the Stockholm International Peace Research Institute, 11 May 1979, published in *Apocalypse Now?* (Nottingham, Spokesman Books, 1980), p. 11 (also available in pamphlet form from the Campaign for Nuclear Disarmament).
6 OTA, *The Effects of Nuclear War*, p. 3.
7 Douglas Hurd, MP, Minister of State at the Foreign Office, quoted in *The Times*, 9 October 1981, p. 8. For a careful statement of the UK government's thinking on deterrence, see Michael Quinlan, 'Preventing War', *The Tablet*, 18 July 1981, pp. 688–691.
8 Peter Blaker, MP, Minister of State for the Armed Forces, quoted in *The Times*, 3 November 1981, p. 5.
9 Quoted by Sir Neil Cameron, 'Defence and the Changing

Scene', *RUSI, Journal of the Royal United Services Institute for Defence Studies*, 125, no. 1 (March 1980), p. 21.

10 Ibid., p. 27.

11 *The Military Balance, 1981–1982* (London, International Institute for Strategic Studies, 1981), pp. 73, 124. Precise figures are: Warsaw Pact, 4,788,000 (of which USSR, 3,673,000): NATO, 4,933,000 (of which USA, 2,049,000); China, 4,750,000.

12 Dale R. Herspring and Ivan Volgyes, 'How Reliable are Eastern European Armies?' *Survival*, 22 (September/October 1980), pp. 208–218.

13 *The Military Balance, 1981–1982*, p. 124.

14 *SIPRI Yearbook 1980*, pp. xxvii–xxix, 222.

15 *The Military Balance, 1981–1982*, p. 124.

16 The phrase is that of Professor Michael Howard in his 'Case for keeping a strong conventional arms capability' (*The Times*, 3 November 1981, p. 13); *The Military Balance, 1981–1982*, p. 126–127.

17 M. Leitenberg, 'Background Information on Tactical Nuclear Weapons', in Frank Barnaby, ed., *Tactical Nuclear Weapons: European Perspectives* (London, Taylor & Francis, 1978), pp. 17, 78.

18 '. . . the Soviet Union is probably serious when she says that any weapon that can hit her is "strategic" ' (Gregory Treverton, *Nuclear Weapons in Europe*, Adelphi Papers 168 [London, International Institute for Strategic Studies, 1981], p. 9).

19 For general comments on this theme, see Frank Barnaby, 'The Danger of Winnable Wars', *New Scientist*, 9 June 1977, pp. 378–379; idem, 'Death Beneath the Waves', *New Scientist*, 27 September 1979, pp. 958–960; Jerome D. Frank, 'When Fear Takes Over', *Bulletin of the Atomic Scientists*, April/May 1979, pp. 24–26; Francis X. Winters, 'The Nuclear Arms Race: Machine versus Man', in H. P. Ford and F. X. Winters, eds., *Ethics and Nuclear Strategy?* (Maryknoll, N.Y., Orbis Books, 1977), pp. 144–155.

20 Listing of wars and interventions, 1960–1980 compiled by William Eckhardt and Edward E. Azar, and cited by Ruth Leger Sivard, *World Military and Social Expenditures, 1980* (Leesburg, Va., World Priorities, 1980), pp. 9, 30.

21 Nigel Calder, *Nuclear Nightmares: An Investigation into Possible Wars* (London, BBC, 1979), pp. 125–130.

22 Mountbatten, 'The Final Abyss?', p. 12.

23 *The Military Balance, 1981–1982*, p. 126.

24 Robert C. Aldridge, *The Counterforce Syndrome: A Guide to US Nuclear Weapons and Strategic Doctrine*, rev. ed. (Washington, Institute for Policy Studies, 1979), p. 24. See also House of Commons, Fourth Report from the Defence Committee, Session 1980–81, Strategic Nuclear Weapons Policy, 20 May 1981, particularly minutes of proceedings, 7 April 1981, pp. 255–274.

25 *World Armaments and Disarmament, SIPRI Yearbook 1981* (London, Taylor & Francis, 1981), pp. 20–45; Richard J. Barnet, *Real Security: Restoring American Power in a Dangerous Decade* (New York, Simon & Schuster, 1981), pp. 25–34.

26 Barnet, *Real Security*, p. 30.

27 Fred Iklé (now [November 1981] us Under-Secretary of Defence for Policy) in testimony before the Sub-Committee on International Security and Scientific Affairs of the Committee on International Relations, us House of representatives, 5 November 1975, cited by Walter Schütze, 'A World of Many Nuclear Powers', in Franklyn Griffiths and John C. Polanyi, eds., *The Dangers of Nuclear War* (Toronto, University of Toronto Press, 1979), p. 88.

28 Ruth Leger Sivard, *World Military and Social Expenditures, 1981* (Leesburg, Va., World Priorities, 1981), p. 6. On the vexed question of comparative East/West Military spending, most authorities, including the International Institute for Strategic Studies, have concluded that NATO (even prior to President Reagan's 1981 budget) has been outspending the Warsaw Pact (see especially the careful study in Sivard, *World Military and Social Expenditures, 1980*, pp. 7, 32–33; also *The Military Balance, 1981–1982*, pp. 5–39, esp. p. 15). What really matters, of course, is not the expenditure but the manpower and weaponry of the two alliances.

29 *SIPRI Yearbook 1980*, p. xvii; Sivard, *World Military and Social Expenditures, 1981*, p. 24.

30 'Every gun that is made, every warship launched, every rocket fired, signifies, in a final sense, a *theft* from those who hunger and are not fed, from those who are cold and are not clothed'. (Dwight Eisenhower, quoted by Philip Noel-Baker, 'Disarmament and Development', in Richard Jolly, ed., *Disarmament and World Development* [Oxford, Pergamon Press, 1978], p. 3.) (italics mine).

31 Goodwin, *Nuclear War*, p. 13.

32 *Statement on the Defence Estimates, 1981* (London, HMSO, 1981), p. 1.

33 Millard C. Lind, *Yahweh is a Warrior: The Theology of Warfare in Ancient Israel* (Scottdale, Pa., Herald Press, 1980); Vernard Eller, *War and Peace from Genesis to Revelation* (Scottdale, Pa., Herald Press, 1981), chaps. 1–4.

34 Presentations, in order of ascending thoroughness, are Myron S. Augsburger, 'Christian Pacifism', in Robert G. Clouse, ed., *War: Four Christian Views* (Downers Grove, Ill., InterVarsity Press, 1981), pp. 81–97; R. E. D. Clark, *Does the Bible Teach Pacifism?*, rev. ed. (London, Marshall Morgan & Scott, 1983); Ronald J. Sider, *Christ and Violence* (Scottdale, Pa., Herald Press, 1979, and Tring, Herts., Lion Publishing, 1980); Jean Lasserre, *War and the Gospel* (London, James Clarke, and Scottdale, Pa., Herald Press, 1962). For a survey of eighteen types of pacifism, including Yoder's own type ('the pacifism of the messianic community'), see John H. Yoder, *Nevertheless: Varieties of Religious Pacifism* (Scottdale, Pa., Herald Press, 1971).

35 Richard J. Cassidy, *Jesus, Politics and Society* (Maryknoll, NY, Orbis Books, 1978), pp. 40–47; John H. Yoder, *Politics of Jesus* (Grand Rapids, Eerdmans, 1972); Martin Hengel, *Victory over Violence* (Philadelphia, Fortress Press, 1973); Luise Schottroff, 'Non-Violence and the Love of One's Enemies', in R. H. Fuller, ed., *Essays on the Love Commandment* (Philadelphia, Fortress Press, 1978), pp. 9–40.

36 Jean-Michel Hornus, *It is Not Lawful for Me to Fight: Early Christian Attitudes toward War, Violence and the State*, rev. ed. (Scottdale, Pa., Herald Press, 1980).

37 Roland H. Bainton (*Christian Attitudes toward War and Peace* [Nashville, Abingdon Press, 1960], p. 119) has pointed out that St Francis's witness was not unequivocally pacifist. For Chelcicky and Fox, see Peter Brock, *Pacifism in Europe to 1914* (Princeton, Princeton University Press, 1972), chaps. 1 and 7. For Trocmé, see Philip Hallie, *Lest Innocent Blood Be Shed* (New York, Harper & Row, and London, Michael Joseph, 1980); André Trocmé, *Jesus and the Nonviolent Revolution* (Scottdale, Pa., Herald Press, 1973). Martin Luther King's views are best encountered in his *Strength to Love* (London, Fontana, 1969).

38 W. M. Abbott, s. j., ed., *The Documents of Vatican II*

(London, Geoffrey Chapman, 1966), pp. 290–294; *The Church and the Atom* (London Press and Publications Board of the Church Assembly, 1948), p. 30; James T. Johnson, *Ideology, Reason and the Limitations of War* (Princeton, Princeton University Press, 1975), pp. 10, 131.

39 Presentations, in order of ascending thoroughness, are: Arthur F. Holmes, 'The Just War' in Clouse, *War*, pp. 117–135; James F. Childress, 'Just-War Criteria', in Thomas A. Shannon, ed., *War of Peace? The Search for New Answers* (Maryknoll, NY, Orbis Books, 1980), pp. 40–58; Oliver O'Donovan, *In Pursuit of a Christian View of War* (Bramcote, Notts., Grove Booklets on Ethics [15], 1977); John Eppstein, *The Catholic Tradition of the Law of Nations* (London, Burns, Oates & Washburne, 1935), pp. 65–122; Paul Ramsey, *War and the Christian Conscience* (Durham, NC, Duke University Press, 1961).

40 Bainton, *Christian Attitudes toward War and Peace, passim.*

41 George Kennan, 'Foreign Policy and Christian Conscience', *Atlantic Monthly*, May 1959, pp. 47–48, quoted by Robert W. Tucker, *The Just War: A Study in Contemporary American Doctrine* (Baltimore, Johns Hopkins University Press, 1960), p. 77n.; John C. Ford, 'The Hydrogen Bombing of Cities', *Theology Digest* (Winter, 1957), reprinted in W. J. Nagle, ed., *Morality and Modern Warfare* (Baltimore, Helicon Press, 1960), pp. 98–103.

42 R. A. Markus, 'Conscience and Deterrence', in Walter Stein, ed., *Nuclear Weapons and Christian Conscience* (London, Merlin Press, 1961/1981), pp. 65–88; Arthur Lee Burns, *Ethics and Deterrence: A Nuclear Balance without Hostage Cities*, Adelphi Papers 69 (London, International Institute for Strategic Studies, 1970), p. 26.

43 John Stott, sermon at All Souls, Langham Place, London, 11 November 1979; printed in *Christianity Today*, 8 February and 7 March 1980, and in *Crusade*, November 1980. Other ethicists in the just war tradition construe the theory more loosely than Stott, and allow for the deterrent effect of the possession of strategic nuclear weapons, and even for the 'discriminate' use of counterforce nuclear weapons (in which the anticipated, but 'unintended', casualties might total 25 million): Paul Ramsey, *War and the Christian Conscience*; idem, *The Just War* (New York, Charles Scribner's Sons, 1968); James T. Johnson, 'Weapons Limits and the Res-

traint of War: A Just War Critique', in Joseph L. Allen, ed., *Society of Christian Ethics, 1980, Selected Papers from the Twenty-First Annual Meeting* (Dallas, 1980), pp. 89–109; Gerard J. Hughes, 'Is the Deterrent Really Immoral?' *The Month*, May 1980, pp. 147–149. For comment on Ramsey's thought, see G. R. Dunstan, *The Artifice of Ethics* (London, SCM Press, 1974), pp. 109–110: 'It would seem that logic here goes beyond moral sense: deaths by the million, foreseen and inevitable but not directly intended, are scarcely easier to contemplate than the same result achieved by direct attack.'

44 For a profound meditation on repentance in the nuclear age, see Jim Wallis, *The Call to Conversion* (New York, Harper & Row, 1981; Tring, Herts, Lion Publishing, 1982).

45 James Fallows, *National Defense* (New York, Random House, 1981).

46 Willy Brandt, ed., *North-South: A Programme for Survival*, pp. 13–15, 119–124; Robert L. Heilbroner, *An Inquiry into the Human Prospect* (London, Calder and Boyars, 1975), pp. 43–45.

47 The term 'military-industrial complex' comes from General Dwight Eisenhower's final address as President of the United States. For illuminating comment, see Neild, *How to Make Up Your Mind*, pp. 55–56, 77–79; Alva Myrdal, *The Game of Disarmament* (New York, Pantheon, 1978), pp. 155–158.

48 Walter Brueggemann, *Living Toward a Vision: Biblical Reflections on Shalom* (Philadelphia, United Church Press, 1976); Colin Brown, ed., *The New International Dictionary of New Testament Theology* (Exeter, Paternoster Press; Grand Rapids, Zondervan, 1976), II, pp. 776–783. Those who speak of the 'peace' which the nuclear deterrent has brought to Europe are thinking in terms of pagan Roman *pax* rather than Biblical *shalom/eirene*.

49 Dale Aukerman, *Darkening Valley: A Biblical Perspective on Nuclear War* (New York, Seabury Press, 1981), chaps. 3–5, 14.

50 Walter Sawatsky, *Soviet Evangelicals Since World War II* (Kitchener, Ontario, Herald Press, 1981), p. 14; Nationwide Initiative in Evangelism, *Prospects for the Eighties: from a Census of the Churches in 1979* (London, The Bible Society, 1980), p. 15.

51 Rabbi Marc H. Tanenbaum, in preparatory documents for

International Conference on the Holocaust and Genocide, Tel Aviv, 20–24 June 1982.

52 *Statement on the Defence Estimates, 1981*, p. 4.
53 *Report on Defence, 1961* (London, HMSO, 1961), p. 3, Cf. the comment by Sir Neil Cameron, then Chief of the Defence Staff, while in China in 1978: 'Our two countries [the UK and the People's Republic of China] are coming more and more together. This must be good, since we both have an enemy at our doors whose capital is Moscow' (*Guardian*, 2 May 1978, p. 1). See also *A Global Strategy to Meet the Global Threat*, intro. by Sir Neil Cameron (London, British Atlantic Committee, 1981), p. 16, which sees Japan *and possibly China* as attached to the nucleus of the Atlantic Alliance for the purpose of 'stemming the Soviet advance in the Third World'.
54 Letter of 28 September 1981 from Michael Randle, Co-ordinator of Alternative Defence Commission, School of Peace Studies, University of Bradford; *Statement on the Defence Estimates, 1981*, pp. 64, 66.
55 For the first fruits of the findings of the Alternative Defence Commission, see Michael Randle, 'Defence without the Bomb', *ADIU Report*, January/February, 1981, pp. 4–7, 11.
56 On 30 May 1970, *The Times*, in a lengthy leading article, gave sympathetic consideration to this approach. Cf. the more recent article in *The Times* on 29 October 1981, 'Nuclear-free, but no pushover'.
57 Adam Roberts, *Nations in Arms: the Theory and Practice of Territorial Defence* (Studies in International Security, 18) (London, Chatto & Windus, 1976).
58 Gene Sharp, *The Politics of Nonviolent Action* (Boston, Porter Sargent, 1973) contains a mass of narrative and analysis and has been the stimulus for a great deal of further research.
59 B.H. Liddell-Hart, 'Lessons from Resistance Movements – Guerrilla and Non-Violent,' in Adam Roberts, ed., *The Strategy of Civilian Resistance* (London, Faber & Faber, 1967), pp. 205, 209, 211. 'National defence through passive resistance' is also the stance advocated in recent years by the American Christian sovietologist who was the architect of 'containment' (George Urban, 'From Containment to Self-Containment: A Conversation with George Kennan', *Encounter*, 47 [September 1976], p. 37). For a recent study see Gene Keyes, 'Strategic Non-Violent Defense: The Construct

of an Option', *Journal of Strategic Studies*, 4 (June 1981).

60 Cameron, 'Defence and the Changing Scene', p. 21.

61 For an example of what a congregation can do, see the story of the Protestant congregation of Le Chambon-sur-Lignon, which under the leadership of André Trocmé engaged in non-violent corporate struggle against the Nazi occupation forces in France and which was instrumental in saving the lives of over 3,000 Jewish people (Hallie, *Lest Innocent Blood Be Shed*).

62 For some suggested routes, see Dan Smith, *The Defence of the Realm in the 1980s* (London, Croom Helm, 1980), chaps. 8-10; Neild, *How to Make Up your Mind*, pp. 125-134.

63 Article II: 'Each non-nuclear-weapon State Party to the Treaty undertakes not to receive the transfer from any transferor whatsoever of nuclear weapons or other nuclear explosive devices or of control over such weapons or explosive devices directly or indirectly; not to manufacture or otherwise acquire nuclear weapons or other nuclear explosive devices; and not to seek or receive any assistance in the manufacture of nuclear weapons or other nuclear explosive devices.'

Article VI: 'Each of the Parties to the Treaty undertakes to pursue negotiations in good faith on effective measures relating to the cessation of the nuclear arms race at an early date and to nuclear disarmament, and on a treaty on general and complete disarmament under strict and effective international control' (Trevor N. Dupuy and Gay M. Hammerman, eds., *A Documentary History of Arms Control and Disarmament* [New York, R. R. Bowker, 1973], pp. 561, 564).

64 *Times*, 28 October 1981, p. 7.

65 The parallel of war with slavery as 'an age-old institution [that] has outlived itself' was advanced by the brilliant German philosopher/physicist Carl-Friedrich von Weizsäcker (*Ethical and Political Problems of the Atomic Age* [London, SCM Press, 1958], pp. 18-19) and has been developed at greater length by R. E. D. Clark (*Does the Bible Teach Pacifism?*, chap 3).

66 The analogy of slavery is central to the inter-church anti-nuclear movement in the United States which is promoting the New Abolitionist Covenant. For information, see *Sojourners*, August 1981, pp. 17–19, or write to *Sojourners*, P.O. Box 29272, Washington DC 20017 USA.

For Further Reading

Dale Aukerman, *Darkening Valley: A Biblical Perspective on Nuclear War* (New York, Seabury Press, 1981)

Roland H. Bainton, *Christian Attitudes Toward War and Peace* (Nashville, Abingdon Press, 1960)

Nigel Calder, *Nuclear Nightmares: An investigation into Possible Wars* (London, BBC, 1979)

Walter Stein, ed., *Nuclear Weapons and Christian Conscience* (London, Merlin Press, 1981)

B   The Christian and Nuclear Weapons

MRAF Lord Cameron
(former Chief of the Defence Staff, Principal of King's College, London)

The great issues of nuclear weapons and the Christian faith are, I am glad to say, being discussed today more thoroughly and sensibly than at any time in the past. Nuclear weapons have been used only twice at Hiroshima and Nagasaki. The shock and horror of those two occasions were enough to indicate that the super-power defence strategic balance had entered a new phase and that the issues of war, weapons and peace would never be quite the same again. The fact is that peace has now been sustained in Western Europe for nearly thirty-eight years, and historically this is a considerable period. The explanation has been that peace has existed on the deterrent effect of the possible use of nuclear weapons – abhorrent perhaps to some Christians but effective, in that people in the countries outside Soviet domination have been able to worship in peace and freedom.

If I were to propose a text for what I have to say it would be this one from Deuteronomy:-

'Only take heed, and keep your soul diligently, lest you

55

forget the things which your eyes have seen' (Dt.4.9 RSV)

My eyes saw the Battle of Britain fought to keep Nazi tyranny from dominating this country. I have seen my friends killed or badly burnt in their fighter aircraft. They were young men, full of life, but conscious of the threat which Nazi Germany posed to their country. I have seen the War Graves in the Western Desert where so many brave and courageous soldiers, sailors and airmen perished in a foreign land, so that their homes might be kept safe. I have been to the Belsen gas chambers and seen in detail Hitler's attempt to exterminate the Jews. I have witnessed the Japanese atrocities in fighting against them in Burma. I have seen the labour gangs in the Soviet Union at first hand. I have seen the recent satellite photographs of the greatest rearmament programme in history being carried out by the Soviet Union. I will not forget what my eyes have seen. But as a committed Christian, though I have forgiven, I am determined that attempts to destroy our freedom to worship God as we like must be resisted, and if pressed to the ultimate, even by the use, or threat of use, of nuclear weapons. I am a man of peace, a dove not a hawk, a multilateral disarmer; but I believe to the depth of my soul that we must defend our Christian way of life. I believe the present Soviet threat is a considerable danger and that we must react to it.

The Soviet Armed Forces today number more than 5 million men. For the past decade this force has grown in size and in the spread of technology quite beyond anything that could be conceived as a reasonable defence posture. All arms of the Soviet Union's Forces have benefitted from their expanding defence budget. They will shortly pull ahead of the United States for the first time in strategic nuclear throwweight. This is a significant psychological factor in the super-power balance.

The Soviet Army now amounts to more than 180 divisions, against 57 divisions of NATO forces. They have some 20,000 artillery pieces and 50,000 tanks. This represents 3 to 1 superiority against NATO forces. Their tanks, the T72 and T80, are more modern and better equipped than their NATO counterparts. They have some 5,000 helicopters for attack, support and air transport. More than 3,500 Soviet and Warsaw Pact tactical bombers and fighter aircraft are located in Eastern Europe – again a 3-1 superiority over NATO. The SS20 mobile nuclear delivery system, each missile having three warheads, is being rapidly deployed in East Germany and on the Chinese border. These missiles have the range capability of hitting all the major cities of Europe and China, but not of the United States. The Backfire bomber force, which is really a missile system, goes on growing and is now capable of attacking targets from a stand-off range of 400 miles. The Soviets continue to give high priority to the modernization of their Inter Continental Ballistic Missile force and their Submarine Launched Ballistic Missile force. The Soviet strategic nuclear arsenal now includes 7,000 nuclear warheads, with 1,400 ICBM launchers, 950 SLBM launchers and 300 nuclear bombers.

This enormous growth of the Soviet Armed Forces is made possible by the USSR's military production base which is expanding at the expense of all other components of the Soviet economy. Today the Soviets have more than 85,000 men fighting in Afghanistan, while Soviet naval forces (which are also expanding rapidly) are deployed in the major oceans of the world. The USSR is gaining increased access to military facilities and is supporting proxy conflicts in Africa, South West Asia, South East Asia, the Western hemisphere, and the Carribean.

What is this tremendous Soviet force expansion all about? Can it really be believed in 1982 that the West has any aggressive designs on the Soviet Union?

In such a world Western governments are not merely entitled but positively bound to protect their people's right to peace and freedom by something more substantial than just good motives and hoping for the best. As

Christians we are surely bound to uphold the essential dignity of individuals against the contempt of human rights demonstrated by the Soviet leadership.

The Ethical Teaching of Jesus

Now, how is the ethical teaching of Jesus to be understood in this situation? It is clear that to think of Jesus as being a pacifist or as teaching pacifism is highly misleading. Pacifism implies a specific programme of action in relation to the state, namely an individual's refusal to serve in the armed forces, and a conviction that all people ought to refuse to do so.

But because of his belief about the overwhelming importance of the Kingdom of God and the necessity of responding to its proximity in an act of total trust and love, Jesus had almost nothing to say about the state and its claims, nor about the whole area of life which comes under the heading of justice. I doubt whether the teaching of Jesus has any direct bearing on the question of pacifism or non-pacifism as we know it.

I feel the works of the 17th Centuary Dutch jurist and theologian Hugo Grotius still remain applicable:

'If the right of . . . defending the citizens by arms against robbers and plunderers was taken away, then would follow a vast licence of crime and a deluge of evils.

Wherefore if the mind of Christ had been to induce such a state of things as never was heard of, undoubtedly he would have set it forth in the clearest and most special words, and would have commanded that none should pronounce capital sentence, none should wear arms: which we nowhere read that he did: for what is adduced to this effect is either very general or obscure.'[1]

The direction to love one's enemy, which presumably includes those who mug old ladies in order to steal their savings, does not mean that such assailants should be

58

allowed to remain free to commit further acts of a similar nature. In order that old ladies may go unmolested, coercive force has to be brought in as a protection and as a deterrent.

The application of these laws requires that we take into account the often brutal realities of life and the many claims that have to be met, not least the necessity of maintaining an ordered justice as the essential condition for the growth of personal life.

From this point of view, agreements limiting arms, conventions safeguarding particular groups of people, attempts to keep the nuclear balance stable, and efforts to make the United Nations more effective, are real, though partial, achievements in inching forward towards the ultimate ideal. They are desperately hard-won attempts to realise in international life the demands of divine justice.

The state is able to represent justice, law and stability because it has a superiority of coercive power. Justice, in so far as it is expressed through law, is backed by the threat of force and can be implemented on many occasions only through the use of force. The only effective way to achieve obedience in many cases is for the state to make use of man's most powerful self-protecting force – his self-interest; and to deter destructive acts by making the consequences fearful.

At this moment, whether we like it or not, stability between the super powers is maintained by thousands of men in Washington and Moscow who calculate and re-calculate the possible effects of every action their respective governments might take.

I feel the two super powers are united in a common goal of avoiding war, and every development which might render the present balance unstable is subjected to searching analysis. Robert Osgood, of John Hopkins University, Washington, has written:-

'What is novel in contemporary crisis management is the intensity of aspiration to exercise a far greater control over those critical junctures in state relations than men have exercised in the past and the confidence that this may be done through exhaustive analysis, imaginative speculation and careful planning for future actions'.[2]

Without being totally optimistic that such a mastery of events can be fully achieved, this description is not an unfit one for ethical man, or Christian man, who is seeking to grow up and become responsible.

One of the unfortunate implications of absolute or even nuclear pacifism is that this whole attempt to manage events in the cause of a just peace is regarded as discreditable. Yet these men, for the most part cautious bureaucrats, acting upon their own and mankind's fearful conviction that nuclear war must be avoided, especially I suggest, deserve the understanding and critical appraisal of other citizens.

It is true that most New Testament scholars, whilst acknowledging some significant points of contact between Jesus and the Zealots, remain unconvinced that he was the leader of an armed revolt. Nevertheless, it is not the foregone conclusion it might once have seemed that even Jesus himself was non-violent.

Granted that Jesus did not advocate armed revolution, is his ethical teaching really to be interpreted as a set of rules which can and ought to be put into effect in a straightforward way? Jesus taught that God himself would bring in the Kingdom, and that this transformation of the whole fabric of human life was already beginning.

Had Jesus's conviction about the imminent rule of God any effect on his ethical teaching? I believe it had, in the sense that if he had known that life would continue for a further 2,000 years, he would have spoken more fully on subjects that he left almost untouched.

Most of the decisions that we have to make require us to take into account the long-term consequences of our actions, and they involve many, perhaps conflicting claims. In particular, there are the moral claims that arise from the necessity of having a just and ordered structure of society, which is the essential pre-requisite for any kind of significant human existence.

But these sometimes clash with the moral claims that arise out of a particular person's individual need. Jesus, with his conviction about the overwhelming importance and nearness of the Divine Kingdom, was able, I suggest, to disregard conflicting claims and the long-term consequences of action, and focus on person-to-person situations. What I am trying to say is that it is wrong in my view to accept totally and blindly that the words and sayings of Jesus 2,000 years ago necessarily apply to the political, defence and deterrence situation of the year 2,000.[3]

War is clearly inconsistent with the Kingdom of God as Jesus spoke of it and lived it. The teaching, life and death of Jesus were concerned with this Kingdom, and not with the governments of a warring world. So the justification of war must be made in terms other that the teaching of Jesus.

The Just War Theory

These terms must be the defence of the State and the freedom to worship God as one wishes. This brings us to the 'Just War theory' and its rules as they have developed down the centuries. First, war must be instigated by lawful authority. Secondly, there must be a just cause; as one such, self-defence is taken for granted. If there is a necessity, a wrong can then be put right. Thirdly, there must be a just intention as well as a just cause. The object of war is to bring true peace, and to punish the aggressor. For nothing is more truly a misfortune 'than the good fortune of offenders by which pernicious impunity is maintained and the evil disposition strengthened'. That is a lovely quotation of Augustine, meaning of course that God looks upon the just and the unjust, and they both seem to do as well as everybody else.

Fourthly, the conduct of the war must be just, and faith

kept, even with the enemy. Aquinas follows in the tracks of Augustine. Luther develops the theme and sees no difference between armies being used for internal peace and those involved in warding off external threats. 'For what is a just war', he asks, 'but the punishment of evil doers and the maintenance of peace?'[4] He sees three possible uses of the sword, and for the 'sword' read nuclear weapons, or whatever. First, to rebel – and this he condemns. Secondly, to quell a rebellion – and this he says is essential. Thirdly, the sword between equals he accepts, but only if one is attacked or to right a wrong. The duty of rulers is to protect their people.

Now let us try to apply the present strategic situation and the Just War rules to the West's defensive posture against the Soviet Union. War would be instigated by a lawful authority in that the states of NATO in consultation would take the decision to go to war (to some extent or other) against an aggressive Soviet Union 'if one or other of their number' had been attacked. They would be legally constituted states making a conscious act. The cause must be assessed as just in that an act of aggression has been made against one or several countries, with Moscow knowing quite clearly that NATO would fight for its freedom.

The just intention would surely be to convince the Soviet Union by an act of defence that their aggression was an error of judgment, that the West's freedom was worth fighting for, and by persuasion and diplomatic as well as military action that they must return to the status quo. The question of punishment for this aggressive act would depend greatly on the situation of the time. On the fourth element of the Just War NATO would have to ensure that the conduct of the war remained just and was not allowed to get out of hand in the pursuit of excessive retribution.

I touch on these theories and philosophies only to show that, since the fall of man, human beings have been at variance with their Creator, and often with their neighbour as well. As a result, there have been wars and rumours of wars, and none of us knows how best to cope. For we live in a sinful world, where sometimes the choice for mankind lies not in black or white, but in two very similar shades of grey. Pacifists of all kinds make appeal to the rights and wrongs of their case and the case against them. They tend to get hooked up on concepts such as right and wrong, black and white.

When dealing with these concepts you can easily distinguish one from the other, black from white, right from wrong. But we do not live in a world of concepts; we do not live in a world where the absolutes are always attainable. Conceptually speaking, it is easy to say that war is wrong. This is what the pacifist does, and then emphasises the wrongness of it. When you get down to the realities, however, you find that the absolute distinction disappears and you are left with 'rightness' being the best possible action under the circumstances. Now this may fall far short of the *concept* of rightness, but it is the best we can do. If, for example, the war against Nazi Germany was evil, yet it was the best thing we could do in the circumstances, then that war in real practical terms was nevertheless right.

The several aspects of the Christian dilemma can be seen in the words and works, I think, of two very famous Anglican leaders, George Bell, Bishop of Chichester and William Temple, Archbishop of Canterbury. Bishop Bell wrote in his book *Christianity and World Order* – 'It is indeed the duty of Christians – of the Church as Church – to exercise the prophetic function, both humbly and impartially declaring where justice lies, and guiding the moral conscience by the application of principles. The Church will also guard and maintain these moral principles in the war itself . . . It should oppose any war of extermination and enslavement, and any measures directly aimed at destroying the morale of the population.[5]'

In this quotation the, dilemma, the heartache and the conflict of the nation (a Christian nation still upholding

Christian principles of morality and charity) are clearly seen.

It may well be that Bishop Bell and the thousands who supported him were right. But there were many others who argued that in a conflict such as World War 2, no civilian could remain outside like a spectator at some gladiatorial contest between opposing forces in uniform. It was also argued by many that if you were a conscientious objector or a pacifist then logically you should not even be allowed to eat the food and wear the clothes that soldiers, sailors and airmen had risked or given their lives to provide.

By the outbreak of World War 2 the evil of Hitler's Nazi regime had identified itself in a way that evil in World War 1 never did. I am not saying that evil in World War 1 never existed. Far from it, but it just did not manifest itself in such a clear-cut way. On the other hand, Hitler's extermination policy against the Jews was clearly and manifestly evil. A man deeply involved in both World Wars was William Temple. He took a somewhat different view from Bishop Bell, identifying to some extent the conflicting sides and attitudes within the Christian Church. Temple saw the Second World War in an altogether different light.

In September 1939 he wrote: 'The prevailing conviction is that Nazi Germany and oppression are destroying the traditional excellencies of European civilisation and must be eliminated for the good of mankind.'[6] Speaking for the Christian conscience, Iremonger, in his biography of Temple, writes 'All the more for this reason, the reason of conscience, he found himself called to vindicate the character of God, and to justify the taking up of arms in the name of the Prince of Peace.'[7] We need to remember this when we come to look at the contemporary Communist threat. In answer to the continual questioning of pacifists, Temple maintained that the pacifist syllogism was too naive in such a complex situation. Was logic, he asked, not the enemy of truth? 'He replied that in a fallen world, the rightness of most acts is relative. To kill is right if at all, relatively, not absolutely; that it can only be right in special circumstances, but in those circumstances it is absolutely right.'[8]

William Temple expounded this idea in a letter to a young friend who was very worried in her conscience in November 1939. He wrote

'in the circumstances killing is right, though I am not denying it is sinful. But we are in a position where the choice is between two evils, so we are involved in an entanglement due to the sin of mankind, including our own, in which the best thing we can do is still a bad thing. Nonetheless, it is still right to do it, because it is the best possible. Where the method of redemptive suffering is possible, and the people concerned are capable of rising to it, it is no doubt the best of all, but there is no way which I can see in which we could redemptively suffer so as to change the heart of Germany and deliver the Poles and Czechs. . . . So once again we have to do the best we can, being what we are, in the circumstances where we are – and then God be merciful to us sinners!'.[9]

I think that is important. So if you are going to suffer, then suffer redemptively. And if you are not going to suffer redemptively, then you have got to think twice about suffering. Now while disagreeing strongly with the outlook of pacifists, Temple never failed to treat them with courtesy and consideration. He transformed the 'cat and mouse treatment' which many conscientious objectors had undergone in World War I into something on a higher plane. To one pacifist he wrote –

'Though you cannot advance the Kingdom of God by fighting, you can prevent Christian civilisation or a civilisation on the way to becoming Christian from being destroyed, and that is what we are now engaged in.

If you look at the New Testament carefully, there can be no doubt that there is a theology of the State as well as a theology of the Church, and that it is our duty as citizens in support of the State to do things that would be inappropriate to do as Churchmen in support of the Church and its cause. The military are therefore quite wrong if they went on to say that therefore Christians ought not to fight.'[10]

The duty to fight is a civic duty which, if the cause is good, Christianity accepts and approves of. But it is not a duty which has its origins in Christianity as such. When questioned by many about the sucessful bombing of the Ruhr dams, Archbishop Temple wrote from Lambeth in 1943,

'the decision whether or not to go to war or to support a country in war, is a desperately serious one. But whichever way it is answered, the answer must be regarded as carrying with it the full consequences. If we answer – No – we ought to have been naturally ready for the establishment of the Nazi regime, Gestapo and all, all the rest of it in Britain, rather than fight. If we answer – Yes – we must be ready for what is required to defeat the enemy other than the inflliction of useless suffering. I think there is no doubt that the bombing of the Ruhr dams was a perfectly legitimate act of war. There is a great deal to be said for refusing to fight, but I think myself that in this case it would be shirking a duty. There is still more, I think, to be said for fighting in support of freedom and justice, but there is nothing whatever to be said for fighting ineffectively.'[11]

The Present and the Future
What then of the present and future situation? Nuclear weapons, we know, are at this moment trained on all the major cities of Europe, the United States and Soviet

66

Russia. Their prevailing presence is even more acute than anything hitherto contemplated.

In his books *The Just War* and *Force, Order and Justice*, Professor Tucker writes that civilian deaths are equally intended, like soldier's deaths, and similarly they become a means to an end. Even if they are only for propaganda purposes they are involved either in a negative way, or a positive way. Civilians vote in governments though not in Nazi Germany or the Soviet Union. Paul Ramsey, the American theologian, in a book called *The Just War*, rightly draws a distinction between intentions and consequences. The intention is concerned with the final end of the war, which, of course, is peace. The consequence is concerned with the morality and means of achieving this state of peace.

Professor Tucker, like Luther and Calvin, argues that the individual has a clear responsibility to the state, and has therefore, in effect, a charge to do anything and everything to defend it. Now that is worth thinking about. The state as such is a close interlocking system of material organisation and power with a body of ideals and principles. 'Destroy the organisation and the power, and you destroy the effective operation of the ideals and the principles.' That quotation comes from a British Council of Churches' report.[12]

Are we not saying, then, that democracy *per se*, would not, could not, exist without structures to establish it and uphold it? And are we not then saying that society, having been based upon these structures, then needs a religious ingredient, injected into it to keep it on a straight path? The trouble is that the steps we have to take today, or at least threaten to take, to uphold the framework of our democratic way of life, are the very steps which contradict the values we are trying to establish. What we are doing is to threaten to kill a large number of people in order to preserve the freedom and safeguard the dignity of the individual.

These are the arguments that are being levelled at all the

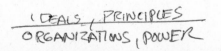
IDEALS, PRINCIPLES
ORGANIZATIONS, POWER

militarists at the moment, and it is right that we should be thinking about them. Perhaps a better way of justifying defence is to say that we are not finally prepared to allow might to be right. Perhaps in the international scene a certain amount of anarchy might be acceptable, so that each individual is accountable to himself or herself for their own actions. What we need, perhaps, is a balance of power. Now this is exactly what we have got, and this has been established over the last twenty or thirty years. The morality of deterrence is as old as the hills. Both shield and sword, as I have said before, are defensive. But they also have a deterrent effect, particularly if they are bigger than those of the side which opposes you.

The nuclear technological situation of the present time precludes there being a defence system capable of withstanding the attack. Intercontinental Ballistic Missiles in hardened sites, or in invulnerable submarines at sea with multi-warheads, ensure the possibility that a least some will find their way to the target. Everything then depends upon deterrence. So what is the morality of deterrence? Is there a 'Just Deterrence'? What is the morality of threatening to put to use that which it would be immoral to use? Paul Ramsey has always argued that because it would be immoral to drop a nuclear bomb on a city, people would tend to doubt if one would ever do so, and so the deterrent value of having it would be lost or at least reduced. Having reached a sort of stand off situation, there has gradually developed a counter-force policy.

It started in the fifties, and grew to maturity in the sixties and seventies, with the concept of tactical warfare being waged on limited targets of military value, and this by all acceptable standards is not necessarily immoral. The very fact that we have target weapons below the counter like Punch and Judy, is a deterrent in itself. Of course, the possibility that we will not use them, does not signify that we might. There is another great deterrent to be taken into account. Nobody wants a country void of people, or the wherewithal to support people. A nuclear desert is a poor prize for winning an expensive war.

So all governments use a good deal of ambiguity in their statements about defence. It gives them room for manoeuvre, because let us be clear that no one wants to commit genocide. Let us hope that governments are as responsible as we give them credit for. But frankly I would be worried about trusting the government of the Soviet Union. I would quote their rapprochement with Hitler in 1940; their treatment of the Polish people in 1945 and again recently; their campaign against the Jews; the Gulags; their attitude to human rights; and so on. Having said this, she is a nation with a great many holy and godly people, and more people will perhaps be at church in the USSR most Sundays than will be in Germany or France or Great Britain. Yet oddly enough, the Soviet Union with all these godly people has its political power invested wholly in the hands of a convinced and committed minority of Communists. This is where the danger and the mistrust lie.

The Communist government causes the West great anxiety, not simply because it has repudiated the Christian ethic root and branch, but because it has thrown out a more natural morality as well. All the moral and religious foundations upon which Western civilisation is built are regarded by the Communists as so much bunk, to be discarded at will. And it is this thought, kept continually in focus, which encourages us to make our choice. If you have sympathy with the Communist, then you have not understood his philosophy, a philosophy which is fundamental to his way of life, namely that everything and everybody is subordinate to what the state finds good. But clearly this sort of philosophy, giving rise to that sort of power, is not to be trusted, and consequently until they are to be trusted we will have to keep them in check.

This means having a deterrent which deters. The only thing the Soviet Union will recognise as a deterrent is something like equal power, the balance of power upon which all our political strategy is based. We are talking

EVERYTHING AND EVERYBODY IS SUBORDINATE TO WHAT THE CORPORATION FINDS GOOD

69

EVERYTHING AND EVERYBODY IS SUBORDINATE TO WHAT THE STATE FINDS GOOD

about facts and facts only. But the result of this policy of deterrence has been a checkmate in nuclear armament. Before World War 2, such a checkmate existed with regard to the use of chemical and biological warfare, and it is of course significant that neither was used in World War 2. Can we not then argue along similar lines with regard to nuclear weapons? I think it is fairly clear that the Soviet Union does not want a nuclear war, for the simple reason that she does not need one in order to promote revolution.

It seems to me, speaking personally, that the Soviet Union is succeeding remarkably well on the political and psychological fronts. She does not need to fight us. The Soviets maintain a nuclear armoury as the supreme threat. We maintain ours as a defence against that threat. In a way it is the wire fence that seperates two cockerels, which march up and down on either side. To remove the deterrent would be to remove the wire fence; the relative peace would be shattered, and both feathers and blood would fly. To be red or dead is an 'easy-come' phrase, which rolls off the tongue in an easy manner, but it conjures up a frightening choice which faces our civilisation. If confronted with the choice to live without any of the things which give life value and make it worthwhile, or to die trying to preserve these things, then I know that for me it is better to die.

Finally, when one asks what is the just function of a fighting service in a country like Great Britain, the answer must surely be that we exist not to make wars, but to prevent them. The pacifists might have the words, but it is the soldiers who give their blood so that peace might be re-established. There are no bigger pacifists than members of the forces, I can tell you. 'When a strong man fully armed guards his own palace, his goods are in peace; But when one stronger than he assails him, and overcomes him, he takes away his armour in which he trusted and divides his spoils.' (Luke 11.21,22; RSV) Let us make sure that our house is well and truly guarded, so that our life and liberty, and our ability to worship in peace, may be kept safe for future generations. And may the God of love, compassion and peace have mercy upon all of us!

Sir Neil Cameron wishes to express his gratitude to the Rev Richard Harries, Dean of King's College, and to the Rev Clifford Jobson, Senior Chaplain, Rhine Army, for the material with which they provided him.

1 Hugo Grotius, *De Jure Belli Ac Pacis Libre Tres* (originally published 1646; this edition: Oxford, Clarendon Press, 1927, Bk 1, ch. 11, para. 6, p. 66).
2 Robert E. Osgood and Robert W. Tucker, *Force, Order and Justice* (John Hopkins Press, 1967) p. 342.
3 Richard Harries, 'The Tygers of Wrath are Wiser Than the Horses of Instruction' *Theology* (September 1972).
4 Robert C. Schultz, ed. *Luther's Works* (Fortress Press, Philadelphia, 1967), Vol. 46, p. 98.
5 George K. A. Bell, Bishop of Chichester, *Christianity and World Order* (Penguin, Harmondsworth, 1940), p. 86.
6 F. A. Iremonger, *William Temple, Archbishop of Canterbury, His Life and Letters* (Oxford University Press, Oxford, 1948), p. 543.
7 ibid. p. 541.
8 ibid. p. 542.
9 ibid., p. 543, see also pp. 66off.
10 ibid., p. 544.
11 ibid., p. 545.
12 *The Era of Atomic Power*, a Report of the British Council of Churches, 1946.

3 North and South: the Economic Debate

Donald A. Hay
(Fellow and Tutor in Economics, Jesus College, Oxford)

THE BRANDT REPORT

(a) *the genesis of the Brandt Report.* One of the most surprising features of the Brandt Report, *North-South: a Programme for Survival,*[1] has been the publishing success of the paperback version launched in early 1980, which has sold over 100,000 copies. Such a circulation is unprecedented for a work on international development issues published in Britain. Even if the level of purchases has not been fully matched by attention to its contents, the Report has imprinted itself on public opinion, and will be regarded as a touchstone for discussions of development issues for some years to come. Not least the Report has been enthusiastically espoused by Churches and Christian-based development groups. The purpose of this essay is to provide an assessment of the Report which will enable Christians to reflect constructively on the issues involved, and to contribute to the development debate in the future.

The idea of an independent Commission to inquire into international development progress and problems was first mooted by Robert McNamara, then President of the World Bank, in early 1977. His suggestion was that such a commission would be able to give fresh impetus to the development debate, and would set the agenda for the 1980s. It would also be timed to appear ten years on from the influential Pearson Report[2] on aid and development, which had had considerable influence in the 1970s (though it never achieved the widespread publicity that has been accorded to the Brandt Report).

By the end of 1977, Herr Willy Brandt, the former Chancellor of West Germany, announced the formation of such a Commission. It came to have 18 members, ten from the Third World, or 'South', and eight from the developed First World, or 'North'. The members were political figures rather than development experts. But they were also chosen for their interests in international issues. Four of the members were former Prime Ministers or Chief Ministers in their own countries. A wide range of political viewpoints was aimed at, but this has not prevented critics from subsequently accusing the Commission of being biassed towards the broad European social democratic tradition to the exclusion of more radical political elements. The work of the Commission emphasised the political element. Over two years the members visited all parts of the world, and maintained contacts with many world leaders. This work is described in some detail in an Appendix to the main Report. But the Commission did not lack expert advice. They interviewed many eminent specialists on international development issues, and they had their own expert secretariat. The Report cannot be criticised for its lack of competence in dealing with the economic issues.

The brief of the Commission was described in the terms of reference '. . . to study the grave global issues arising from the economic and social disparities of the world community, and to suggest ways of promoting adequate solutions to the problems involved in development, and in attacking world poverty'. The work was to encompass the record of development, the prospects for the world economy, and 'roads to a new international economic order'. There is an unmistakable air of urgency about these terms of reference, particularly in their emphasis on the provision of 'adequate solutions'. The Report was not intended as another recital of the debates about development policy.

The Report was unveiled at the end of 1979, and published in early 1980. The first impressive fact is that it was a unanimous Report. There were no minority reports, and no dissenting notes. Given the range of views represented by Commission members, this was no mean achievement. Even more remarkable was the fact that unanimity was not achieved by compromise or 'fudging' on the important issues. On the contrary, as we will see below, the Report espoused a very clear line of analysis and recommendations. Third, the style of the Report merits comment. It is not a work of great literature, and is perhaps rather too long. But it is written in a popular style without the usual paraphernalia of economic reports. There are no tables or figures, no graphs and no formal economic analysis. The interested lay person could read it without difficulty. Furthermore it is not a coolly analytic work. On the contrary, there is an element of passion with which it is presented, not least in the introduction by Willy Brandt. It seeks to convince and persuade. It is a political 'tract for the times'.[3]

(b) the content of the Brandt Report. The content of the Brandt Report is just as remarkable as the style. Since 1964, the Third World delegates at successive United Nations Conferences on Trade and Development (UNCTAD) have formed themselves into a group called the Group of 77. Its membership now includes well over one hundred Third World countries, and they have developed a set of proposals which they have consistently argued for within UNCTAD and without. These proposals are frequently referred to as the search for a New International Economic Order (NIEO). They include seven major areas of concern to the countries of the Third World.

The first is that priority in international aid and development should be given to the poorest countries, or least developed countries as defined by the United Nations. These countries are characterised by very low income per capita (less than $100 per head at 1970 prices), very little manufacturing industry, and high rates of illiteracy. They are located in Central Africa, south of the Sahara, and in a belt that stretches from the non-oil countries of the Middle East across South Asia and into East Asia. Their particular feature is a heavy dependence on agriculture to support their populations, coupled with difficult environmental conditions. Major problems arise from climatic uncertainties, including prolonged exposure to drought, and from endemic diseases such as malaria, sleeping sickness and bilharzia. Not surprisingly, their potential for development does not make them attractive for private development finance, or even for loans from international development agencies. The returns are too uncertain, and results may only be achieved in the very long run. But the needs of the population are acute, and something must be done. The call is for much more financial assistance, on a grant basis, or on concessional terms, and for development of production techniques specifically designed for the difficult environmental conditions.

A second priority of the NIEO is an attack on world hunger, by giving greater attention to questions of food supply. Malnutrition is estimated to affect some eight hundred million people in the world. Unfortunately, the majority of these people are located precisely in those low income countries that do not have the capacity to import food when domestic production is insufficient. During the 1960s and early 1970s, grain stocks in the United States were allowed to run down, as a result of policy changes by the United States Government. These stocks had previously been used to stabilize the world markets for grains. The effects of the policy change were first seen in the years 1972 and 1973, when droughts in Africa and poor domestic harvests in the Soviet Union, led to a sharp rise in wheat prices. The consequence was that many poor countries were literally priced out of the world markets, with serious food shortages as a result. The demand of the Group 77 is that such crises should not be allowed to recur, and they proposed and argued for an International Grains Agreement, which would provide for a reserve stock to be maintained. The finance for this was to be provided by the major developed countries. The Third World simply lacked the financial capacity to undertake this task themselves. But such a programme would be insufficient, in view of rapid population growth, to solve the food problem. So the Group of 77 stressed a new priority to be given to agricultural development, to reduce the dependence of poor countries on imported food.

A third area of concern of the NIEO is with trade in commodities. Many Third World countries are highly dependent on exports of commodities (agricultural and mineral) to earn foreign exchange for development and growth. For some of these commodities there has been a long term decline in price relative to prices of manufactured exports from the North, though this depends much on the particular commodity and the time period over which comparisons are made. Much more immediately, commodity prices have been subject to wild swings in recent years, with deleterious effects in the exporting countries, which are never able to predict accurately their foreign exchange earnings. Finally, Third World countries have noted that their share in the commodities market is limited to production. Processing, marketing and distribution in the North are the preserve of Northern firms, often multinationals, whose activities are protected by tariffs and non-tariff barriers to trade which inhibit Southern producers from competing in these areas. A consequence is that the producers on average receive only twenty-five per cent of the final price to consumers of the commodities they produce. The NIEO proposals to cope with these perceived problems fall under three heads. First, although it is generally conceded by experts that little can be done to affect the long term shifts in relative prices, there is a certain degree of optimism that it may be possible for a group of Third World producers to emulate the success of OPEC in forming a cartel to reduce production and raise prices. Second, the Group of 77 has pressed for effectively financed International Commodity Agreements with a view to maintaining stocks and stabilising prices. Insofar as the remaining price swings affect producing countries, there are demands for special international compensatory financing arrangements to help by providing financial aid to a country when it is adversely affected, which can be repaid when the particular commodity price later recovers. Third, the Group of 77 has urged various measures to enable producer countries to embark on processing and distributing their commodities, and to ensure free access to consumer markets in the North.

A fourth emphasis of the demands by the Third World for NIEO is in the area of industrialisation. The share of Third World countries in world manufacturing output has increased slowly during the 1970s. They have also had some success in increasing their share of world trade in manufactures. But this has been limited to a small group of eight countries, often referred to as the newly industrialising countries (NICs) which include Brazil, Korea, Taiwan and Singapore. Their export growth has been severely checked in the latter part of the 1970s by increasing protectionism in the North, which is specifically directed at products which are the potential exports of the Third World e.g. textiles, clothing, electronics and steel products. While the NICs are possibly capable of diversifying their exports to overcome the restrictions imposed by tariffs and quotas, the prospect is not so good for new Southern countries seeking to establish manufacturing production for exports. The Third World has not been slow to point out the inconsistencies of the North, which, through the conferences of the General Agreement on Tariffs and Trade, have systematically reduced the barriers to trade between Northern economies. But the same countries have been deaf to the requests of the Third World for more liberal trade policies in respect of their potential exports. The solution proposed by the Group of

77 has been a planned reduction in protection, linked to positive policies in the North to facilitate 'adjustment'. Adjustment is necessary in so far as new Third World producers will displace domestic production in the North, so that Northern workers will need to switch into new industries.

Fifth, the Group of 77 has consistently advocated, in UNCTAD and elsewhere, effective international control over the activities of multinational or transnational companies. This has been linked to the question of the transfer of technology to the Third World. The former objective, that of control over multinationals, would be met by an internationally agreed code of conduct, to strengthen the bargaining position of host countries, and by international cooperation in the area of corporate taxation. In respect of transfer of technology, it is recognised that multinationals often control the technology that the Third World needs in order to develop its own resources and productive potential. But there is concern about the terms on which this is available, and that it may not always be appropriate to the conditions of the South. Both these difficulties could be overcome by developing the capacity of the South to do its own research and development, so as to reduce its reliance on multinational technology, and to provide more appropriate technology.

The Group of 77 has always been highly critical of the institutions and international agreements that constitute the international monetary order. That order was created in 1944 by the Bretton Woods agreement. It provided for the International Monetary Fund (IMF) to regulate international monetary relationships. The agreement was directed particularly to the problems of the advanced industrial countries, each of which agreed to maintain a stable value for its currency, in return for the right to obtain short term finance from the IMF, should it suffer a temporary set back in its balance of payments. Unfortunately the agreement did not foresee the post-war growth in international trade, and did not provide a means for increasing international reserves to match that growth. In the event, the United States filled the gap by running balance of payments deficits, and other countries were content to add to their reserves in the form of dollars, especially while the United States continued to promise to redeem dollars for gold from its own reserves at a fixed price. This pattern broke down in the early 1970s when world confidence in the dollar began to ebb, and a number of countries, including Britain, were unable to maintain a fixed exchange rate. The Group of 77 has argued that much more rapid progress should be made in moving from national currencies to truly international currencies, like the Special Drawing Rights of the IMF, to finance international trade. Understandably, they complain of a system which has enabled the richest country in the world (the United States) to import more than it exports by the simple device of printing dollars. Of all the countries in the world they have the least need of this particular privilege. Special Drawing Rights could be allocated to the Third World (via a mechanism called the SDR-Link), who would then have some of the erstwhile advantages enjoyed by the Americans. This is but one part of their analysis. The other is their argument that the IMF was created for developed countries, and its policy has been dictated by advanced countries. Thus the IMF has tended to treat requests for assistance from Third World countries, for help with short term balance of payments problems, on the same basis as requests from Britain or other advanced economies. The terms for assistance have therefore sometimes included a requirement that a Third World country adopts highly restrictive fiscal and monetary policies, which have caused hardship and distress. But, as the Group of 77 maintain, changes in policy are unlikely to come about while the IMF remains a 'rich man's club' with decisive voting strength lying with the advanced countries. Hence their demand is for more Southern participation in the policy making of the IMF.

Finally, the demands for a New International Economic

Order have included a solution to the problems of Third World indebtedness. Since the early 1970s the amount of Official Aid has fallen far short of the development needs of the Third World. The result is that those countries have turned more and more to private banks to finance their development programmes. However this debt has grown to such proportions that there are doubts about their capacity to service the interest and repayments. So private lending will not provide for the needs of the 1980s. The problem with development aid has not only been its quantity, but also the terms on which it is offered. The particular complaints are: that aid is only available for specific investment projects, and not for flexible use in broad development programmes (e.g. in agriculture); that aid is often tied to purchases in the donor country; that too much aid is given unilaterally, rather than multilaterally, thus making its continuing availability subject to the changes in foreign policy of the donor; and that the flow of aid is not sufficiently predictable to enable a Third World country to plan its development even in the medium term (up to five years ahead). The Group of 77 have therefore asked not only for more aid, but also that these questions concerning the *form* of aid should be dealt with. There have, for example, been a number of proposals for international 'taxation' (e.g. levies on the exploitation of sea bed minerals, or on the export of arms), which would accrue automatically to a multilateral aid granting body.

These seven areas have been the subject of intensive pressure in UNCTAD and other United Nations fora for the past 15 years, and have generally been resisted by the North, despite some progress on particular points. The astonishing fact about the Brandt Report is that it accepts in broad outline not only the analysis, but also the demands for a NIEO in all seven areas (Chapters 4, 5, 9, 11–14). It is certainly not as radical as many Third World commentators would have liked,[4] but the intellectual case is completely accepted. Indeed there is virtually nothing new in the proposals of the Brandt Report. All the main policy ideas have been around for several years, and have been much discussed.[5, 6, 7]

To the NIEO proposals, the Brandt Commission has added five other areas of analysis. The first two refer to matters that are *internal* to the countries of the South. They are the need for population policy, and a call for internal economic policies more directed to disadvantaged groups and regions. Population policy should include plans to keep population growth within the capacity of the economy to provide an adequate standard of life. The problems caused by migration, both within the South, and by international migration, are also singled out for attention. The section of the Report on policies internal to the South (Chapter 8, 'The Task of the South') has only seven pages on economic policy which implicitly favour development directed to basic human needs in the area of housing, food, employment, education and health. The rest of this section explores the possibility of economic cooperation between countries of the South. A further two chapters of the Report deal with international issues that were judged to have particular links with development in the Third World, armaments and energy. Armaments are discussed further below. On energy, the Report draws attention to the difficulties created for non-oil producing Southern economies by the rise in the world price of oil. Its recommendations include a programme of search for new energy sources, orderly transition from oil and long term measures of conservation of non-renewable resources. But this is not much more than what has been forced on North and South alike by the circumstances. The only new proposal was for a new energy affiliate of the United Nations with specific responsibility for these programmes.

Finally, the Brandt Commission addressed itself to the problem of obtaining international agreement on issues concerning development and aid. While accepting that negotiation had to be conducted within the framework of the United Nations, the Commission expressed concern

81

about the difficulties of reaching agreement within such a large body. The inevitable grouping of countries into bargaining groups (like the Group of 77 in UNCTAD) was seen as making progress more difficult. Such groups tended to adopt the positions of their most radical (or conservative!) members with the outcome that negotiations quickly became deadlocked. So the suggestion was that recourse should be made to occasional summits of a small, but representative, group of countries which could generate a new impetus to negotiations at the level of the United Nations. It was precisely such a summit which was proposed by the Commission as the first step in the consideration and implementation of their proposals. The proposed summit took place in Cancún, Mexico in October 1981.

(c) the Cancún summit: aspirations and results. The Cancún summit counted on the presence of 22 world leaders from both North and South. Willy Brandt's own hopes for the summit were that it would make progress on an emergency programme for the years 1980-85, and produce a commitment to a long term process of implementation of the Report's proposals. The 'emergency programme' included a massive transfer of financial aid to the non-oil countries of the South, to overcome their immediate problems of debt and need for development aid, an international energy strategy, and a global food programme. It was also proposed to take the first steps towards reform of the international system.

However, the results fell rather short of these aspirations. Early in the summer of 1981, President Reagan cast gloom over the planning for the summit by insisting that the talks should be only informal, without detailed negotiations on specific proposals, and without any formal statement or communiqué. The gloom deepened about a week before the conference when he made a speech extolling the virtues of free market capitalist development, and implicitly rejecting all the major recommendations of Brandt. Not surprisingly the Third World participants were angered and dismayed. Whatever the United States' view on the detailed proposals of Brandt, it made little sense to accept an invitation to such a summit without making at least some effort to be open minded and flexible. Diplomatically, it was a serious blunder, which will only add to the deep seated antagonism towards the United States in the Third World, where the power of the United States in international economic affairs is greatly resented.

Not surprisingly therefore the summit produced very little of what had been hoped for. The excuse proffered was that the governments of participants in the summit were not in a position to commit non-participants. The comment of Mr Edward Heath in the House of Commons' debate refuted this specious argument: 'It was always accepted that no member of the Cancún summit could commit other countries, but there was nothing to prevent them commiting themselves'. The most that was achieved was an understanding of the importance of the issues involved. The British Prime Minister, Mrs Margaret Thatcher, was reported as much impressed by an Indian proverb quoted by Mrs Gandhi; 'I complained of having no shoes until I met a man with no feet', in comparing the economic problems of Britain and India. The long-run results of the Cancún summit can only be indirect, via a greater commitment to progress in the usual United Nations negotiations.

Despite this apparent failure, the Brandt Report is likely to be an important document for international economic discussion in the coming years. Church leaders, charitable development agencies and world development groups have made great use of it in Britain to bring pressure to bear on the government, culminating in a mass lobby of Parliament in May 1981. It is therefore important that we look critically at the Report, and determine which parts of it we can go on using, and which parts it would be wise to discard.

We have already seen that the Brandt Report was essentially a political document, and not a technical report on the causes and origins of international inequality. But the political arguments presuppose a certain technical analysis, and therefore invite a critical analysis. Broadly speaking, the Report seeks to convince Northern leaders that they should take action on the proposals for a New International Economic Order. The arguments can be summarised under two headings. The first heading might be 'arguments from doom': the suggestion that failure to act will result in some irresistible disaster that will engulf not only the South but the North as well. The second heading is 'arguments from mutual economic interests'; the proposition that it is to the advantage of the North to act on Southern demands because it is in their long term economic interest. These arguments are thought to be more persuasive than the traditional arguments from humanitarian concern, or, more robustly, from the ethical demand for justice.

(a) arguments from doom. The subtitle of the report is 'A programme for Survival'. This theme of survival in the face of impending catastrophe is emphasised in Willy Brandt's personal introduction. He wrote (page 13): 'Our report is based on what appears to be the simplest common interest: that mankind wants to survive, and one might even add has the moral obligation to survive.' And (page 27): 'Global questions require global answers: since there is now a risk of mankind destroying itself, this risk must be met by new methods.' The particular disasters that are foreseen are war, irretrievable ecological damage and the collapse of the international economic system. It is only fair to add that the main text of the Report is less alarmist in its expositions of those fears.

Warnings of these kinds are oddly attractive to Christians, especially Evangelicals, who like to see in them modern equivalents of the prophecies of the Old Testament or of the apocalyptic literature of the New Testament. But there are two vital differences. First, the writings of contemporary secular prophets contain very little moral content. The breakdowns described are due to physical or social malfunctioning. A proper Christian response would be to ask how these predictions are compatible with a doctrine of God's providence in creation and in human history. Second, the modern prophets are inherently optimistic about man's capacity to cope with the problems identified, so long as the matter is properly understood. More knowledge, more commonsense, and a little bit of compromise should let mankind safely off, and the disaster can be averted. But for the Old Testament prophets the vital ingredient was repentance. Christians should therefore think Christianly about the predictions of secular doomsters, and be suspicious of the humanistic solutions which are offerred to the problems which are foreseen.

Our particular criticism of Brandt is not however along these lines. Rather it is that Brandt failed to argue a convincing case for linking various world problems to the North-South issue. This is not to deny the importance of these problems for the future of mankind, but merely their relevance for the case that the Brandt Report was making. The failure to sustain a convincing case is clearly seen in the case of war and armaments. The report comments (p.13): 'The relationship between armaments and development is still very much in the dark.'[8] The implicit point in the Brandt Report is that tensions between North and South are a complicating factor in East-West antagonism, and that 'Third World countries could easily become theatres of conflict between nuclear powers'. But as P. D. Henderson has remarked,[9] there is no evidence at all to link the limited wars and conflicts of recent years with issues of international economic justice or even world hunger. The conflicts in South East Asia have been inspired by ideology, the wars between Israel

85

and her neighbours have a religious and ethnic significance, and many other disputes can be traced to long standing conflicts over territory or other rights. This is not to deny that international inequality and hunger could spark off a future war. But it seems unlikely on *a priori* grounds. The fact is that the poor are powerless, and the hungry die very quietly. The world has already suffered severe famines affecting more than one country, and inequality is no new phenomenon. The voice of the poor is little heard mainly because it is the voice of the *rural* poor. Urban poor are kept sufficiently fed by anxious governments, and any trouble is quickly put down by repressive police forces or armed services.

The second 'argument from doom' attempts to link the North - South question to the possibility of ecological disaster. This is not spelled out in the Report, except in references to the destruction of the environment in some Third World countries by the indiscriminate cutting of forests for fuel, especially in the poverty belts of Africa and Asia. Curiously, there is no mention of the destruction of the Amazon forests in Brazil, which is likely to have much more serious effects on the world ecosystem. However this is an argument that can generate undesired responses. For example, some might argue that it would be better to discourage Southern development in order to keep the total strain on the ecosystem at a tolerable level. A parallel argument, more espoused by Third World ecologists, is that the real problem is Northern overdevelopment, not Southern underdevelopment. The North cut down its forests indiscriminately even centuries ago. The North by its profligate consumption of fossil energy is producing carbon dioxide that cannot be absorbed by the world's biosphere. Yet it is the North that points an accusing finger at the poor South, and demands to know why the trees are being cut down. At most then, the ecological argument is a highly complex correlative of the North-South problem: it gives no particular incentive to its solution. Exactly the same point can be made about the use of non-renewable resources.

The third 'argument from doom' considers the possibility of a total collapse of the world economic system. Two lines of thought are discernible. First, a number of large Third World countries, like Brazil, maintained their pace of economic development in the mid 1970s, despite the strain on their balance of payments from the oil price rise, by borrowing substantially in private world capital markets. Their willingness to do this reduced the impact of the oil price rise on the world economy, since most Northern economies cut back severely in order to balance their external account, thus inducing depression in the advanced economies. However, by the end of the 1970s the debt of these Southern countries had reached such proportions that there was a real fear in world financial markets of a default on obligations. The result would be a collapse of the world banking system with serious consequences for the stability of the entire capitalist world. But this sequence of events is somewhat doubtful. World bankers have been largely successful in bringing pressure on Third World debtors to adopt highly restrictive internal policies. There has been little default, though extensive rescheduling of debts has occurred. Nor is there much prospect of a collective default by a group of major debtors within the Group of 77. Individual economies are too dependent on imports to make that a real option. The second line of thought evident in the Brandt Report concerns the effect of the oil price rise on inflation and depression in the North. Here is one area, where the South, in the shape of OPEC, has a certain amount of leverage over the North in the world economy. However one may doubt whether OPEC will ever be in a position to cause catastrophic damage in the world economy by unpredictable price rises. The shocks of the mid 1970s were very considerable, and the North has 'survived' (though not, of course, without a degree of trauma). The international capitalist system is in fact strong and sufficiently flexible.

To sum up, it seems that the attempt of the Brandt Report to inject urgency into North-South discussions by predictions of dire long term prospects, with all the rhetoric about survival, is quite unconvincing.

(b) arguments from mutual economic interests. We must now turn to the alternative argument, the argument from mutual economic interest, which is, if anything, a more important element in the Commission's thought. It attracts a whole chapter of the main Report, and is much more characteristic of it, than the arguments from doom of Willy Brandt's introduction. The argument is *prima facie* highly reasonable. If it can be shown that a particular policy change is in the interests of both parties, North and South, in the sense that they both stand to gain, then why not make that change? We will show later that this argument is less than fully Christian, in that the Christian ethic also speaks of the sharing of the benefits. For the moment, it suffices to comment that it is the question of sharing of gains that explains something of the failure of Brandt's arguments to be fully convincing. Mutual gains models, especially models of trade, can give very unequal gains to the parties to a particular transaction. A number of examples from Brandt will illustrate the point.

The Commission states the case for stabilising commodity prices, along the lines advocated by proponents of a NIEO. Many Third World countries are highly dependent on exports of primary commodities. A particularly extreme case is that of Zambia which in the early 1970s earned ninety-four percent of its foreign exchange by the export of copper. The price of copper in world markets has experienced severe fluctuations. The Report quotes a peak of $3034 per ton in April 1974 falling to $1290 per ton by the end of the same year. On annual terms this represented a fall in foreign exchange earnings of some forty-five percent. (Compare this with the oil 'shock' to Western Economies in 1974, where the impact effect was less than a sixth of this amount.) Not surprisingly, the

88

South has advocated international agreements to stabilise the prices of commodities along the lines we described above. But the gain to the North would be minimal. Major commodity users in the North already operate privately in established commodity markets, and are accustomed to looking after themselves. Fluctuations in individual commodity prices are not significant in the balance of payments of highly diversified industrial economies. So the North sees no advantage, and considerable costs, in intricate international commodity schemes. There is also considerable doubt about the efficacy of such schemes.[10]

A similar difficulty besets the argument for trade and against protectionism in the North. Southern industrial exports are hindered by protection, usually in the form of non-tariff barriers, such as quotas, in the North. If these barriers were removed, the South could export more and earn more foreign exchange. Given the constraint of balance of payments problems on their growth, the South are likely to spend any additional foreign exchange to purchase advanced goods, especially capital goods, in the North. There is therefore, in the North, a run down of sectors that match Southern exports, but are not able to compete, and expansion of those sectors that provide the additional Southern imports. Northern workers have to switch jobs, but job losses and gains should be roughly matched. The gain to the North is higher income from more productive workers in advanced sectors, and lower cost supplies of traditional industrial goods. But the gain is only realised in the long run. In the short run, Northern Governments see employment loss in traditional sectors coming on top of world wide depression, and they calculate the real costs of adjustment policies. In particular, the Brandt Report underestimates the sensitivity of Northern democratic governments to the pressure of quite localised and specific industry pressure groups. This pressure is particularly effective where the industry is located in a limited number of cities, and Parliamentary representatives are elected from small geographical constituencies. The textile industry in Britain is a case in point.

An important element in the Brandt Report is the proposal for immediate 'massive' transfers of financial aid to the South by the North. This proposal is addressed to the problem of world recession, which stems originally from the rise in the price of oil. Countries of the North have tried to cope with oil deficits by cutting domestic consumption to reduce imports. The effect of all countries doing this together has been to drive Northern economies into a depression of the dimensions of the 1930s. The situation has been alleviated only by continued growth and development in the South, which borrowed heavily to maintain its expansion. But, as we have seen, that growth is now impeded as the South reaches the limit of its borrowing capacity. The solution proposed by the Report is a direct application of the Keynesian policy analysis of depression. The objective is to reactivate the world economy by *giving* the Southern economies the foreign exchange that they need to continue with their development. This would reverse the situation of the post war years, where as W. A. Lewis has shown,[11] the 'engine of growth' was the advanced economies of the North, which pulled along the world economy. Unfortunately, the timing of this proposal coincided with a switch to a more monetarist thinking on macroeconomic policy in most of the advanced economies, and especially in the United States and Britain. In a monetarist analysis, such financing of Southern development would be inflationary on a world scale, and should therefore be avoided at all costs. That is not to accept that the monetarists are necessarily right in their prognosis. Many economists of a more Keynesian approach believe that the Brandt proposals would work. But at the very least Northern gains from the policy are not self-evident to Northern governments. Even if Keynesian analysis won wider acceptance, it is not clear what is to be gained by an indirect reflation via the South, with uncertain consequences, rather than a direct reflation of the

Northern economies in the conventional manner.

Our conclusion is that the arguments from mutual interest, based on assessment of economic gain to the parties involved, are unlikely to be persuasive for Northern governments. So we are forced back to reliance on moral and humanitarian arguments, which are acknowledged in the Brandt Report, but are not thought to be sufficiently powerful to achieve the radical changes which the Report is seeking. It is to a specifically Christian statement of these arguments that we now turn.

RESTATING THE CHRISTIAN MORAL ARGUMENT.

There are two important Biblical themes which are relevant to our discussion. The first is that of man as steward of the created order and as a worker. In Genesis 1, the story makes it clear that the created order is a stage for human history. Man is described as being in the image of God. It was the custom of kings in the Ancient Near East to set up images of themselves in lands that they conquered. The images signified dominion. So man in God's image implies, among other things, God's dominion over his creation. But that dominion is exercised by man as a trustee or steward. The created order is to be subdued and controlled by man's work. Work is a part of man's nature and vocation. It is alluded to before the Fall: man is told to till and to keep the Garden of Eden. The Fall brings disorder into man's work, and makes it a toil and a burden. But that distorts, rather than destroys, the original vocation to work.

Work is not possible, however, without access to resources. Man is placed in the created order, to work with the materials provided. This is most clear in an agricultural society, where access to land is the prerequisite of effective work. For this reason, when the children of Israel enter the promised land, a parcel of land is assigned to each family in perpetuity. Family land cannot be sold, and that which is lost through debt has to be returned every fifty years at the Jubilee when all debts are cancelled. The linking of work and resources in the New Testament is seen most clearly in Jesus' parable of the servants and the talents in Luke 19. Each is given different talents with which to work, and has to give an account of his work to his master in due course. Initial endowments are not necessarily equal, but at least each one has something with which to work. It is important to note that this parable was told to correct an impression that the Kingdom of God was to appear immediately, which could have given rise to an attitude that the creation order of work could be abandoned. The implication of the parable is exactly the opposite. Further, we should be wary of interpreting the talents *only* in the sense of 'spiritual' gifts. It is surely not without significance that the parable is placed immediately after the story of Zacchaeus with its emphasis on repentance for the wrong use of wealth and money.

The second theme is the obligation of the rich to provide for the poor and needy. In the Old Testament the first defence against poverty was undoubtedly provided by giving each family access to land and hence productive work to do. But that defence may fail: a family may become temporarily landless through debt, or it may lose its productive workers (the case of widows with young children), or a person may be a stranger without rights to land. In each case the rich are instructed to share their abundance with the less privileged. It is this context that gives rise to some of the most difficult teaching of Jesus about poverty and riches, as, for example, the parable of the rich man and Lazarus, or of the sheep and the goats at the Final Judgement. The rich are not condemned merely for their insensitivity and lack of compassion. The situation of the rich man and Lazarus should never have come about if the teaching of the Law had been obeyed, since presumably Lazarus' family would have had access to land.

The primary Christian principle to be applied is *justice*

in the access to resources. Compassionate giving is intended for those cases where conditions make impossible the exercise of responsible stewardship, by access to resources. It is no good giving generously to the poor if our other actions effectively preclude them from exercising a proper stewardship in productive work.

APPLYING THE CHRISTIAN MORAL ARGUMENT.

Before we can apply this Christian moral argument we need to understand the causes of international inequality. The Brandt Report is not very good at giving an overview of the causes. There is a tendency to deal with policy areas one at a time, and to move rapidly into policy recommendations. The unity of the Report comes from the consistent policy that is proposed, and the arguments put up to persuade governments to act on the proposals. That North and South economies reflect the unified problems of a unified world economy is assumed rather than demonstrated.

(a) understanding inequality. One element in comprehending international inequality is to understand the principles of operation of a market system like the international economic system. The two principles are quite simple. First, income in a market system depends on capacity to supply. Second, consumption depends on income. These two principles do not aspire to be much more than truisms, but they are very illuminating in particular applications. Thus a primary cause of poverty in the Third World is that people do not have access to resources, and having nothing to work with, they produce nothing and thus have no income. For example, much rural poverty in Asia and Latin America is directly linked to landlessness. Land is concentrated in the hands of a few, and many of the rural population are without land. In Africa, the problem is somewhat different, since there is access to

land, but the environmental conditions make its use extremely difficult. This points to the fact that natural resources are not likely to be sufficient in themselves for production. The need for 'access' extends to education and technical knowledge, to appropriate technology, *and* to a culture based on hope, and not despair about the possibilities for economic development. This is particularly the case for urban poverty. As the example of Hong Kong illustrates, these elements can make up substantially for a lack of natural resources. Christian *justice* demands that the question of access to resources be given priority.

The second principle of a market economy is that consumption depends on income. This can be dramatically illustrated from A. K. Sen's work on famines.[12] He shows that a root cause of many famines is not the lack of food, but the lack of money with which to buy it. On a world basis, this may be applied to the markets in the main food grains. When harvests are less than expected, shortages tend to push up the price of grains in world markets. The consumers in the North grumble about the higher prices that they have to pay. But the poor are simply eliminated from the market through inability to pay the market price. This is precisely what happened in 1972-3, and the outcome was that many people in Third World countries starved. The ethical defect of this situation is that the distribution of consumption is based on ability to pay, rather than a principle of sharing. It is worth emphasising the structural nature of the evils involved in the situation. Individual consumers in the North are probably quite unaware of the consequences of their capacity to pay higher prices in situations of shortage at existing prices. Certainly it is stretching credibility to argue that they are individually responsible for starvation somewhere in the world. But the consequences of the system as a whole are, in this instance, apalling evils. A structural evil demands a structural solution.

However, the fact of international inequality cannot be attributed only to the impersonal workings of the economic system. There is also the fact that the North has used its power to determine North-South economic relations to its own advantage. The Brandt Report has been much criticised for its imprecise use of the term 'power'. Part of what is meant by the term is simply 'the power of the purse' which we have just described – the capacity to preempt other buyers in world markets by bidding a higher price. But power goes beyond that to power to determine the international 'rules of the game'. An example can illustrate this point. In September 1981, the Reagan Administration expressed forcibly the opinion that the World Bank should no longer lend on concessionary terms to a number of more developed Third World countries, including Brazil. The argument was that such countries were capable of raising funds in private capital markets, and could (or should) pay full market interest rates. A matter of days later the World Bank proposed a change of policy to this effect. There was consternation and anger among Brazilian experts and government officials. They had been given no warning that such a policy change was contemplated, and had had no opportunity to make representations on the matter. Also, such a change in policy was thought to require approval from a full meeting of the members of the IMF. But, regardless of the merits or demerits of a particular proposal, the fact is that once the United States has decided on such an issue, they have no difficulty in getting it formally accepted. Exactly the same inequality of power is perceived by the Third World in many other areas such as commodity trade, trade in manufactured goods and the operations of multinationals. Too often the object of the exercise of such power is to protect Northern interests against Southern demands.[13] The effect is usually to deny to the South full exercise of responsible stewardship over the resources that they have.

(b) the quest for international economic justice. The biblical position is that the authorities in society have the responsi-

95

bility for the pursuit of justice (or more accurately, right-ing injustices) between citizens. But what of international issues? The response of Northern governments, particularly with the problems of inflation and economic depression, has been expressed by the attitude that they must 'put their own house in order' before they can heed the appeals of the South. Such an attitude may be politically attractive in a nationalistic sense, but there is little doubt that it is morally wrong. Rather, the stance in international affairs should be determined *as if* there existed an international body acting on the principle of justice between citizens. In other words, there are principles of international behaviour that go beyond the point of national self-interest. A 'put our own house in order first' response to the problems of international inequality and world hunger is inadequate on any Christian assessment of moral responsibility.

This suggests that Northern churches would be right to stress moral arguments in seeking to persuade their governments. But are these likely to succeed where the arguments from doom and from mutual interest have failed to carry weight? First, we should note that moral arguments have to be put, whether or not repentance is expected. A failure to convince is not necessarily a demonstration of inadequacy. Second, we should add to the moral argument a specifically Christian dimension, which is the dimension of judgment. God will judge those who in their affluence ignore the pleas for justice from the poor, the needy and the oppressed. James 5.1–6 eloquently sums up a wealth of biblical teaching, from both Old and New Testaments, on this theme. This prophetic dimension is not often heard in the pronouncements of Christian Churches and organisations on issues like those raised in the Brandt Report. One wonders whether it is just too embarrassing to try to speak to highly secular political authorities in these terms.

As far as the specific policy proposals are concerned, the Northern churches should stress those changes that seek to enable the people of the Third World to exercise responsible stewardship of the resources they have. In practical terms, that means aid to build up their productive structure, and measures to open Northern markets to their goods. However much one may criticise the specific estimates of the Brandt Report, there is little doubt that a very large increase in multilateral aid would be of great benefit to the developing economies of the South. It is sad that at the time when Brandt was suggesting a target of 0.7 per cent of GNP as an interim target for aid, the UK government is systematically reducing our commitment to a target of 0.38 per cent in 1985. But there is little point in strengthening the productive capacity of the Third World, if at the same time protectionism in the North cuts out those products from Northern markets. Access to Northern markets for semi-processed commodities and raw materials, and for traditional industrial goods is the other priority.

(c) action on economic justice within the South. We have already noted that the Brandt Report has a section on 'The Task of the South', but that it concentrates as much on international economic issues *within* the Group of 77, as on internal policies of the countries concerned. This simply avoids an issue of critical importance. Any sensitive observer of much of the Third World has to note the gross inequality of incomes *within* many Southern economies, the misallocation of investment resources to prestige projects with little social benefit, and the manipulation of economic policy to their own advantage by small political and economic élites. The North-South dichotomy often exists in even sharper contrast within the South. Hence there are serious doubts whether all our best efforts at an international level will trickle down to the poor and disadvantaged within the South. The gains may well reach no further than an already rich ruling élite. The naivety of the Brandt Report on this point has already attracted criticism. But we should also note that it raises a problem

for the moral argument as applied to international economic relations.

This point can be met only by emphasising the need for action by the churches within the Third World. In much of Latin America, Africa, and even parts of Asia, the evangelical churches are stronger numerically than they are in Protestant Europe. Yet they are largely silent on the critical social and economic issues of the development of their societies. For that, the attitudes of the modern missionary movements, until quite recently, must bear much of the blame.

(d) the life of the Church. However there is a prior problem in applying the moral argument spelt out above. The biggest difficulty is that we have not begun to apply it to ourselves, within the church. It is as if we were early nineteenth century Christians trying to persuade the Government to abolish the slave trade, and excusing ourselves for having one or two slaves at home. That is not the kind of inconsistency that would have been found in the life of a Wilberforce or a Shaftesbury. Our personal lifestyles, and the luxury of our churches, are uniquely at variance with the example of our Founder, who, as far as we can tell, had no possessions, who urged his hearers to live light to possessions, and whose immediate followers had all things in common. Poor Christians from the South would find it all very puzzling. Northern Christians save themselves embarrassment since poor Christians seldom come to see. Sadly, many Third World Christian leaders who do come to the North belong to the same privileged élites that are strangely indifferent to inequality within their own countries. They follow the example of their Northern brethren in belonging to churches that are insensitive to the teaching of Jesus about riches and poverty.

The moral case will also carry much more conviction if the Church demonstrates its willingness to use its own resources, however inadequate they may be to the task, to put ethical precept into practice. This is no more than the practice of obedience to the moral arguments that we put. There are immensely encouraging signs that the Church in the Third World is beginning to be active in development, linked to evangelism and Church growth. The book by Maurice Sinclair, *Green Finger of God*, is but one of a number[14] dealing with this issue. It is based on the experience of rural development in Northern Argentina in the last decade, and describes a major project seeking to provide adequate economic conditions for the Indians of the Chaco, many of whom are Christians. A number of advantages of the Church for this work are apparent. First, the Church is often in touch with the poorest people in society, who benefit least from traditional development schemes, which seldom 'trickle down' so far. Second, the presence of the living Church can often provide an essential catalyst, giving a sense of hope and purpose to communities, which in J. K. Galbraith's graphic description resist development because of cultural 'accommodation' to poverty.[15] Third, the Church can often provide experts who bring both the love of Christ and expertise to what can be a very difficult task in inhospitable surroundings.

The Church is a relative newcomer to this field of work, and has much more experience in the rural rather than the urban context. But the potential is enormous, and we should expect the work to grow over the next twenty years. That growth will require both people and money. People are best recruited in the Third World, if at all possible. But they need training. Maurice Sinclair's suggestion of a Christian development university[16] is worthy of serious consideration, as a centre not only for training, but also to do research and provide expert advice. The other ingredient, money, is going to be required on a massive scale. This highlights a paradox that Christian development agencies currently stress that their main constraint is personnel not money. But there are reasons for this apparent paradox. First, the number of projects is still very few in comparison with the potential, and this will certainly change. Second, the level of financial expectations is low. Agricultural development projects do not typically look to Christian agencies for the money with which to buy land, relying on secular aid agencies or government grants of land. Very large projects involving land purchase are not generally presented, because the applicants judge that there are limits to what is 'reasonable' to ask. Third, urban projects, of which there will be more in the future, are likely to be more expensive; land, basic services and construction tend to be more costly. Perhaps the idea of a development university should be considered in conjunction with an international development fund, with budgets running into hundreds of millions of pounds donated by Northern Churches, and not just the millions which Christian development agencies presently collect and distribute. Such a fund would evaluate requests for finance put up by *national* Churches in the South. The policy and evaluations of such a fund should be controlled as much by the South as the North, to avoid the sense of dependency that is often created by relations between Northern Christian development agencies and their Southern applicants. The Northern churches must be prepared to trust their Southern brethren much more, in the responsible stewardship of financial resources delivered to them.

Unless the Christian church is prepared to implement a radical programme in its own international life,[17] our moral arguments do not even deserve to be heard, and our moral advocacy will fail.

1 *North-South : A Programme for Survival* Report of the Independent Commission on international development issues under the chairmanship of Willy Brandt. (Pan Books, London and Sydney, 1980).

2 *Partners in Development* Report of the Commission on International Development (The Pearson Report) (New York: Praeger, for the World Bank, 1969).

3 P. D. Henderson. 'Survival, Development and the Report of the Brandt Commission' *The World Economy* vol.3 no.1 June 1980, pp. 87-117.

4 M. Wionczek, 'What (if anything) can be done with the Brandt Commission's Report?' *Development and Change* vol.12, 1981, pp. 145–163.

5 W. M. Corden, *The* NIEO *Proposals : A Cool Look* Thames Essay No 21 (London, Trade Policy Research Centre, 1979).

6 D. A. Hay 'Christianity and International Economic Justice' in R. Sider, *ed.*, *Lifestyle in the Eighties: an Evangelical Commitment to Simple Lifestyle* (London: Paternoster)

7 J. Bhagwati, *ed.*, *The New International Economic Order: The North South Debate* Cambridge, Mass. MIT Press 1977).

8 There is, of course, a moral case about the scale of military expenditure in relation to spending on development, which the Report makes quite powerfully. But that is a different argument.

9 Henderson op. cit.

10 K. Laursen 'The Integrated Programme for Commodities.' *World Development* vol.6, 1978, pp. 423-435.

11 W. A. Lewis, 'The slowing down of the engine of growth' *American Economic Review*, 1980, vol.70, pp. 555-564.

12 A. K. Sen, 'Starvation and exchange entitlements' *Cambridge Journal of Economics*, 1977, vol.1, pp. 33–55.

13 This is not to deny that OPEC, representing a largly Southern interest, has been able to inflict considerable damage on Northern economies by the exercise of their monopolistic power. But such capacity for the exercise of power by the South is the exception rather than the rule.

14 (a) M. Sinclair, *Green Finger of God* (Paternoster, Exeter, U.K. 1980).

(b) P. Batchelor, *People in Rural Development* (Paternoster, Exeter, U.K. 1980).

(c) R. Sider, ed., *Evangelicals and Development* (Paternoster, Exeter, U.K. 1980).

15 J. K. Galbraith, *The Nature of Mass Poverty* (Penguin: Harmondsworth, Middx. 1980).

16 M. Sinclair, op.cit. p. 114.

17 A. Nichols, *An Evangelical Commitment to Simple Lifestyle: Exposition and Commentary* Lausanne Occasional Paper No.20 (Minneapolis, Minnesota. World Wide Publications 1981).

Suggestions for further reading.

A. I. MacBean and V. N. Balasubramanyam, *Meeting the Third World Challenge* (London, Macmillan for the Trade Policy Research Centre, 2nd edition, 1978) is a readable general introduction to development issues and policies.

The *Brandt Report*[1] itself is essential reading. It was extensively criticised in a series of articles in *Encounter*, December 1980, and a lively debate ensued in subsequent issues. More technical discussions of the proposals for a New International Economic Order are to be found in Bhagwati ed. op.cit.[7] and Corden op.cit.[5] A sharply dissenting viewpoint is expressed in P. T. Bauer *Equality, the Third World and Economic Delusion* (London, Weidenfeld and Nicholson, 1981), especially in Chapters 4-8 and 10. Specifically Christian commentary is available in R. Sider ed.op.cit.[6] Sinclair op.cit.[14] and Batchelor op.cit.[14] are excellent accounts of the possibilities and difficulties of church-based rural development work in the Third World.

4 Energy and Environment: the Ecological Debate

Dr Ian Blair
(Atomic Energy Research Establishment, Harwell)

Today, most of us – at least in the developed countries – enjoy a standard of living beyond the wildest dreams of our forefathers. We live in houses with a level of comfort which in earlier generations was available only to a privileged few. We live longer and have better health care than the majority of our predecessors, and our food supply is ample and varied. We have access to a wide range of manufactured goods, at prices which most of us can afford. The basis of our high standard of living has been our industrial development over the last century or so, and that industrial development has been possible because of the availability of cheap and abundant supplies of energy.

Because it is comparatively recent, it is perhaps easy to overlook the significance of the industrial phase of man's development. It has meant that for the first time in history the ordinary person has had the opportunity to escape from grinding agrarian poverty. The pages of history tend to be dominated by the lives of the wealthy minority of previous generations. Look a little deeper, however, and we find that the common life of people in pre-industrial times was hard, brutish and short, as it still is in many countries of the Third World.

The benefits of industrialisation were not immediately apparent to the ordinary person, however. There were severe social problems created by the shift from an agricultural to an industrial society. People who for generations had lived in small communities with a well established social structure did not find it easy to adapt to life in large impersonal conurbations, with no societal precedents on which to base their new lifestyle. So it took some time for society to adapt, and also to develop the mechanisms which would ensure a more equitable distribution of the newly created wealth. These are processes which continue to the present and are by no means yet complete.

Nevertheless, created wealth there was, and by comparison with earlier generations stretching back to the birth of our race, wealth in incredible abundance. And it all depended on energy, driving concentrated and controllable power sources which multiplied by many hundredfold the power that man could develop from his puny frame.

History of mankind's use of energy

Such then has been the importance of the availability of energy for human development. It may perhaps be instructive at this stage to sketch in simple outline the history of mankind's use of energy down the ages, and to see how our increasing demand for energy has affected our environment.

For primitive man, the only power source he had available was that of his own muscles. With this he had to gather or hunt for his food, after the invention of agriculture to till the land, to build his shelter and to move himself around. All his efforts had to be devoted merely to his survival, and after he had passed the peak of his physical strength in his mid-twenties, his chances of doing that decreased with each passing year.

Eventually he came to realise that although he might be the most intelligent creature on earth, he was by no means the strongest. He gradually developed the skill of using his superior intelligence to train larger and stronger animals to work for him. This enabled him to till more land and hence grow more food; to move larger pieces of wood and stone and hence build a more substantial shelter; and by riding on his animals' backs to travel over much greater distances.

Thus far, man's energy requirements were in tune with the annual cycle of nature. The basic 'fuel' he was using was the food eaten by himself and his animals. This came from each year's crops – the concentrated sunlight of a season's growth. Indirectly he was using the power of the sun, and averaged over a year he was in balance with nature. The energy he could collect from his annual crop supplied his energy needs for that year.

Then man discovered the benefits of fire. He had been familiar with fire for a long time, of course. He had seen the devastating effect of forest fires, and the threat they posed to the existence of his community. Over the generations, man had developed a healthy respect for, indeed a fear of, fire. It was a major step in his advancement when he learned to control this fearsome phenomenon and turn it to his advantage. With it he could protect himself against predators, keep himself warm through the long winter months, cook his food, thereby making it more digestible, fire clay to make building bricks and domestic utensils, and eventually smelt the ores of metals. Now he could avail himself of a new technology, providing him with the tools and implements which were vastly superior to any that were previously available.

The fuel to feed his fires came almost exclusively from wood, obtained from trees in the ample forests that surrounded him. The use of wood as a fuel marked a significant change in his relationship to his environment. Whereas previously he had been in balance with the annual cycle of nature, he was now for the first time in a position to use resources at a rate faster than that at which nature could replenish them. It takes several decades, perhaps a century, to grow a tree. Man could chop it down and burn it in a matter of days. While his numbers were small, and his demand for fuel modest, his effect on the natural woodland was small. Over the centuries, however, the sophistication of his civilisation increased, resulting in a corresponding increase in his demand for fuel. Also, as this enabled him to support a larger population, his numbers increased as well, thus multiplying further his total energy demand. So his demand for wood as a fuel grew inexorably, and he began systematically to deforest vast areas of the planet.

It was, in fact, an eventual shortage of wood in the sixteenth century which led man to start using another fuel – coal. Coal is formed by the action of heat and pressure on long-dead living matter which has become buried under the earth. For that reason it is sometimes referred to, quite correctly, as a 'fossil fuel', for it is the fossilised remains of what lived and grew on earth aeons ago. The natural processes involved in producing coal must operate over a long timescale – a timescale measured in millions of years – so for all practical purposes coal is a non-renewable source of energy. When man started mining coal he was quite literally beginning to dig into his energy capital.

Coal is a very concentrated energy source, and can be used to drive powerful machinery. A capital resource it might be, but man made good use of this accumulated capital. He used it to fuel the industrial revolution which eventually, we saw, led to a dramatic rise in the living standards and material well-being of his rapidly expanding population.

Towards the end of the nineteenth century man discovered another fossil fuel – oil. Like coal, oil is also a concentrated form of energy, but being a liquid rather than a solid, it is much more flexible, and much easier and cheaper to win from the earth, to transport and use. So, shortly after its discovery, and when its potential had become appreciated, demand multiplied rapidly, and the scramble for further and larger supplies began. Some of these new discoveries of oil were in parts of the world with well-established traditional societies, whose cultural background was very different from that of the industrialised world. The cultural shock, which the need for oil made upon them, led to severe political upheavals which have yet to be satisfactorily resolved. Such was the growth in the demand for oil, that by 1960 it had replaced coal as the principal fuel of the industrialised world.

More recently, man has started to exploit another of the earth's energy supplies – uranium. This metal, along with the other heavy elements, was created by the forces that formed the earth and the solar system some four and a half billion years ago. There are no natural processes on earth to increase the amount available, or to replenish what man uses. So, like the fossil fuels, uranium forms part of our energy capital. Like them, once used it is gone for ever. Mind you, a little uranium goes a long way, because it is the most concentrated form of energy that man has yet discovered – something like a million times or so more concentrated than even the fossil fuels.

So we see from this simple summary how man has developed over many millenia, more rapidly over recent centuries, and yet more rapidly still over the last few decades, from primitive beginnings to his present level of material comfort and sophistication. To do this he has needed ever-increasing amounts of energy in ever-more concentrated form. And to get this, he has had to dig deeper and deeper into his reserves of energy capital. Now anyone who lives on his capital knows – and the rest of us can easily imagine – that one cannot go on this way indefinitely.

The Energy Problem
This brings us to the energy problem. It is many-faceted, but for convenience we shall discuss it under three headings: the availability of energy, its price, and the environmental impact of its extraction and use.

Those of us who live in the industrialised world have become accustomed to a high material standard of living. What is more, we have come to expect that standard to rise continually year by year. Throughout the 1950s and 1960s annual growth rates were typically 4–6 per cent, and this era of high growth went on for so long – almost a human generation – that we really came to believe that this was the new norm; that economic growth would continue at this rate, so that material standards would continue to rise; that we had at last discovered a way of solving the problem of poverty; and that things must inevitably get better and better.

The vast majority of mankind, however, living in what we choose to call the Third World, has a material standard of living which is deplorably low – in most cases so low as to be an affront to human dignity. In an attempt to quantify the discrepancy between rich and poor, let us look at the annual per capital energy consumption in various nations, a parameter which roughly correlates with material living standards. To do that, let us define as a convenient unit of energy the ton of coal equivalent (tce), which is the weight of coal equivalent in energy terms to the fuels used of whatever type. In the USA, the annual per capita consumption of energy is about 12 tce; in a western European nation such as Britain it is about 6 tce; whereas in a typical Third World country consumption is only about 1 tce per capita per year.

Quite naturally, the poor nations of the world are trying desperately to raise their own living standard to something approaching ours. It is right and proper that they should do so, and basic humanity dictates that those of us who live in the developed world should encourage them.

So we have a developed world committed to economic growth, and a developing world doing its utmost to catch up. Let us examine the energy implications of this situation. Interesting studies[1] have been done of what might be called the limiting case. They have attempted to estimate the resources required to sustain a fully industrialised world. Not surprisingly, they give quantitative support to what we might have guessed intuitively – it cannot be done. The earth cannot supply the material resources in general, and the energy resources in particular, to sustain a fully industrialised world – specially one committed to continual enconomic growth. Multiply this by the fact that the world's population is still increasing – most forecasters agree that it will almost double within the next 30 years or more, though we may be able to start containing it thereafter – and one then begins to realise the enormity of the catastrophe which threatens to engulf us.

So we have an energy availability problem – a mismatch between the aspirations of mankind in both the developed and the developing world and the ability of the earth to supply the energy to meet those aspirations. We can already see signs of the impending crisis, and most predictions suggest that we have a time span of about a generation or so in which to act to avoid it. Should we fail to take effective action, and attempt to continue down the road we have been taking, the feedback mechanisms of the system will force a solution upon us – a solution which may be far from pleasant; the present phenomena of stagnation in the West and starvation in the Third World may be but harbingers of worse calamities to come.

The availability problem is most apparent over the fuel which supplies the majority of the energy consumed by the industrialised nations – oil. The public first became aware of the oil problem with the dramatic events during and following the Yom Kippur war in the autumn of 1973, but the signs were already visible long before that to those who could read them. In an energy review paper in 1962[2] it was shown that about a decade previously the rate of extraction from the oil fields of the USA, at that time the world's largest producer, had for the first time exceeded the rate at which new discoveries were being made. This transition is significant in the life cycle of a non-renewable resource, in that beyond it the reserves will continually decrease, as has been the case with indigenous US oil since that date. The same significant transition took place for the world's oil supply as a whole towards the middle of the 1970s.[3]. So we must now regard oil as a depleting resource. To illustrate the position more dramatically, the world must find an oil field the size of that under the North Sea or that originally discovered in Texas *every year* just to keep up with its present demand. We will presumably continue to make new finds of oil, but they are unlikely to be on that scale.

We can, of course, in many applications, provide substitutes for oil, either from our energy capital such as coal or uranium, or from our energy income which arises principally from the daily inflow from the sun, but that brings us to the second aspect of the problem. It is not just the availability of energy that concerns us, but its availability at an acceptable price. It was not just the ample supply of oil in the 1950s and 1960s that permitted us to achieve such a large rate of economic growth, but also the fact that it was so cheap. Throughout those two decades the world price of oil in actual money terms remained virtually constant. This means that in real terms – taking account of general inflation over the period – its price was continually falling. The five-fold increase imposed by OPEC towards the end of 1973, which triggered off the economic recession that is still with us today, merely brought the price of oil into line with what it would have been if it had kept pace with inflation over that period. It demonstrated the sensitivity of our industrial society to the price of energy.

So then, as well as an energy availability problem, we also have an energy price problem. Anything we now try to use in place of oil must inevitably be more expensive than oil was then – otherwise we would have been using it already – so we have to ask what the effect will be of this higher price of energy on our industrial way of life. At the present time, in a nation such as Britain, we spend about 5 per cent of our GNP on supplying ourselves with energy. Should the price of energy double in real terms, our economic system could probably adapt to that, provided that the rise was not too rapid; but it certainly could not tolerate a tenfold increase, as that would mean that we would be spending about half our income on energy. It also underlines the point that it is not sufficient merely to identify new sources and to calculate the amount of energy which is in principle available from them; if the price of that energy is unacceptably high, then for all practical purposes it is not available to us.

There is a third aspect of the energy problem, namely environmental pollution. The industrial activity involved in extracting our fuels from the ground, and also that required to convert these fuels into useful forms of energy, can have a deleterious effect on our environment, and also on the health both of workers in these industries and also to a certain extent of the general public as well. Coal mines, uranium mines and oil fields all have their problems in this respect. Large hydro-electric schemes have a marked effect on the local ecology, and if the dam bursts – and sometimes dams do burst – the consequences could be, and indeed have been, tragic[4].

When fossil fuels are burned, poisonous gases such as sulphur dioxide, carbon monoxide and the oxides of nitrogen are released. Also, large quantities of carbon dioxide are produced. This gas is not poisonous. But if we discharge too much of it too quickly into the atmosphere, it could have a disastrous and irreversible effect on the world's climate – the so-called 'greenhouse effect'.[5] This arises from its optical properties, in that it transmits the shortwave electromagnetic radiation in the visible part of the spectrum which falls on the earth from the sun, but it absorbs the longer wavelength infra-red radiation which is normally re-radiated by the earth's surface back into space. The mean temperature of the earth results from a delicate balance between these two energy flows. Therefore the introduction into the atmosphere of significant quantities of a substance which can interrupt the out-flow without affecting the inflow would lead to a rise in the earth's temperature. One does not need much of a rise to start melting the polar icecaps, with a consequent rise in mean sea level, leading to extensive flooding on the highly populated lowland areas of the world.

The concentration of carbon dioxide in the atmosphere is a measurable quantity, and there is no doubt that it is rising. At present it constitutes 335 parts per million of the atmosphere, compared to its pre-industrial level of 290 parts per million. What is less well understood is the concentration level necessary to trigger off the greenhouse effect. Clearly more research needs to be done on this complex but vitally important problem.

Nuclear installations, be they power stations or other plants forming part of the nuclear fuel cycle, discharge radioactivity into the environment[6] – only in insignificant amounts perhaps under normal conditions, but potentially in very much larger amounts should there be a serious accident. Also, the fission of uranium produces radioactive waste which has to be isolated from the biosphere for a considerable period of time.

There has been much public concern expressed over the safety and environmental implications of nuclear power. I have discussed these issues in some depth in a recent book[7], to which I can refer interested readers. Since to discuss them in the same detail here would unbalance this paper, I shall restrict myself to a discussion of some general studies which have attempted to relate the hazards of nuclear power to those associated with our more traditional fuels such as coal and oil. The methodology of these studies is to estimate the number of deaths that might be expected to occur both in the short- and the long-term from a year's operation of a 1000 Megawatt power station, fuelled alternatively by coal, oil and uranium. In each case the effects of the full fuel cycle are included, from the extraction of the raw material, through its use, to the ultimate disposal of the waste products. As well as the effects of the normal operations of the appropriate industries, allowance is also made for those of accident conditions.

The results of the most recent study,[8] which is in general agreement with those of earlier studies, are that the expected number of deaths from producing the previously defined amount of energy from coal are in the range 0.5 to 2.5, from oil 0.2 to 1.2, and from uranium 0.1 to 0.8. This then enables us to view the hazards of nuclear

power in perspective. It is by no means the most dangerous method of producing energy – in fact it is rather less so
than coal or oil.

What is disturbing about the public concern over nuclear power is not the fact that it exists – that is perfectly
right and proper – but rather that it should so dominate
public thinking that it detracts from concern over the
hazards of other energy sources, many of which are far
more serious.

Such, then, is the nature of the energy problem. For as
long as man's use of energy was small compared to the
available economic reserves, and for as long as the pollution produced by his use of energy was small compared to
the capacity of the environment to absorb it, there was no
serious cause for concern. But it is the sheer scale on which
man now uses energy that is at the root of the energy
problem, compounded by the impossibility of supplying
energy on the very much larger scale that would be
necessary to sustain the kind of world society that our
present philosophy, in both the industrialised and the
developing countries, encourages us to strive for. At the
moment it is just a problem; it has not yet become a crisis.
But the writing is clearly written on the wall, and we
ignore it at our peril.

Our response to the energy problem

Thus far we have talked about the present situation and
how we came to find ourselves in it, and we have been able
to do so from a position of approximate ethical neutrality.
Once we move on to consider our response to the energy
problem, however, such neutrality is no longer possible.
How we respond must inevitably depend on our beliefs
about the natural world and man's relationship to it.

Christians base their attitude on the so-called 'cultural
mandate' to be found in Genesis 1 and 2. Here we read that
although man is an integral part of creation, he occupies a
unique position in being created in God's image. This
implies both certain privileges and certain responsi-

113

bilities. In the context of our present discussion, it implies that we have an obligation to make full use of the energy resources of the natural world, in order to improve our common well-being, but that we should do so in a responsible and caring manner. It is a source of deep regret to Christians that the overwhelming majority of those who drive our economic system seems to be unaware of this cultural mandate; and, of those few who are, not many seem to regard it as relevant to their commercial decisions. The driving force behind industrial progress has not been a noble desire for the common betterment of mankind, but rather the baser human characteristics of selfishness and greed. However, the reality of the ecological crisis is becoming more visible with each passing day, and one therefore has reason to hope that necessity, together with that other human characteristic, self-preservation, may impose general acceptance of what Christians have been proclaiming for many centuries – that man is the custodian and steward of the earth and not its outright owner.

Our cultural mandate obliges us to make a much better job of our husbandry of the earth's resources than we have done so far. It also, I believe, puts an obligation on those of us who live in the developed world to rethink our basic attitudes to industrial society – a theme which we shall develop later.

It is unquestionably true that we in the western world have become extremely profligate in our use of energy. During the era of cheap and plentiful energy, we acquired some very bad habits which we must now make a determined effort to break. A few years ago a detailed quantitative study was published[9], which demonstrated the many ways in which we could make much more economical use of our energy resources. Although this study has received detailed and justified criticism[10], mainly over the practicality of some of the measures proposed, this should not obscure its main message – the magnitude of our present energy extravagance and the enormous potential for energy conservation.

I stress this point because this is an area in which individual Christians can exercise their own responsible stewardship of the earth's energy resources. We are, each of us, the ultimate users of the energy that our energy industries produce. Decisions, therefore, on how much is used, and whether or not it is used wisely and effectively, must be taken by each of us individually. We have to decide whether or not to insulate our homes, change to a more energy-efficient form of transport, instal more energy-efficient equipment in our homes or place of work, and generally avoid wasting energy unnecessarily. There is widespread agreement that we in Britain ought to be able to reduce our energy consumption to 80 per cent of what it would otherwise be by the year 2000 if we adopt practical and cost-effective energy conservation measures. It is a reasonable target, but to achieve it wise decisions have to be taken by each of us.

Turning now to the supply side of the energy equation, we noted earlier the vulnerability of our major fuel – oil. Hence the principle of wise stewardship dictates that we should be reducing our dependence on it by turning to other fuels where possible. First, let us consider coal, a fuel of which we already make extensive use. World coal reserves are about ten times those of oil in energy terms. We in Britain find ourselves particularly well blessed, with about 300 years' supply at our present rate of use. At the moment we extract about 130 million tons of coal each year, which supplies about 40 per cent of our primary energy demand. A reasonable target to set ourselves by 2000 AD would be 150 million tons per year, with a corresponding reduction in the amount of oil which we would otherwise have to use. To achieve this, however, mines would have to opened in rural areas, some of outstanding natural beauty. Wise and responsible planning would be needed, therefore, to extract this coal with minimal environmental disturbance.

Next, consider uranium. This fuel already supplies over 10 per cent of our electricity in Britain, and could well be supplying 30 per cent by the end of the century, again with a consequent reduction in the amount of oil which we would otherwise need to burn. Apart from electricity production, uranium has no other commercial use, whereas both coal and oil have a wide range of energy uses and some non-energy uses as well – as a feedstock for the petrochemical industry, for example. It would seem to be sensible stewardship, therefore, to make extensive use of uranium to generate electricity, thereby releasing coal and oil for other purposes.

To those who would argue that we should leave uranium in the ground where it is, let me say this. God created uranium, as he did all the other elements, and placed it on the earth in such quantity that in energy terms it is even greater than the quantity of coal. He has also given us the intelligence to work out how to use it to produce energy. If he did not intend us to use it for this purpose, why did he put it there? The situation reminds me of the parable in Matthew 25 about the man who entrusted his property to his servants in his absence. On his return it was the servants who had made good use of what had been entrusted to them who received his commendation, whereas the one who buried what had been entrusted to him was severely reprimanded. I believe that we risk being similarly reprimanded if we leave in the ground such an abundant energy source as uranium which God has put there for us to use. Of course we must use it wisely and responsibly, as we must all God's bounty, but I know of no moral precept or biblical principle which prevents us from using it at all.

What desperately concerns people, of course, is the fact that uranium can also be used to make weapons of terrifying destructive power. But is there any virtue in not using uranium for peaceful purposes simply because it can also be used to make weapons? Can we prevent its use for weapons simply by not using it for peaceful purpose? The answer to both these questions is 'no'. Man is faced with perhaps the greatest moral challenge in his history. God has created uranium and placed it on the earth. Man has discovered how to use it, either to supply himself with considerable amounts of energy with which to improve his lot or to make weapons of such power that for the first time he has the capability of destroying himself. Which will he choose? Unfortunately, there is no way he can avoid the challenge. Uranium exists, and no amount of wishful thinking will make it go away. We have discovered how to use it, and we know of no way of 'undiscovering' things.

Oil, coal and uranium are all non-renewable sources of energy; they form the bulk of our energy capital. I can see no ethical objection in principle to using the non-renewable source, provided that it is used wisely and we prepare for its eventual depletion. There are other sources of energy – as yet largely untapped – which are either renewable or which use resources which for all practical purposes are inexhaustible. If we are to restrict our time horizon to the year 2000 AD which is the title of this book, then we must discount them all, for there is just not enough time between now and then to research, develop and deploy them. However, perhaps on this occasion we can permit ourselves a slightly longer view.

The first of these is nuclear fusion, the process which provides the sun and the stars with their prodigious energy. The basic fuels for this energy technology are deuterium – a heavy form of hydrogen – and the light metallic element lithium, both of which are in plentiful supply. Indeed nuclear fusion could supply man's energy needs at their present level for millenia. However, it is proving to be a difficult technology to master, and even on the most optimistic predictions it is unlikely that it will be providing us with significant amounts of energy before about the middle of the next century. As yet we have no idea as to its cost. It would be the supreme irony if we were to master this difficult technology, only to find that the energy it produced was too expensive to use. However, the prize is so enormous that it would be irresponsible not to continue to strive for it.

117

Next, there is the energy available in the rise and fall of the tides, deriving from the gravitational attraction of the moon on the oceans of the earth. The technology required to exploit this energy is fairly well established, although the scale is considerably larger than we are familiar with. Present estimates indicate that the economics are just about acceptable, and so a number of schemes – for example the Severn Barrage – are being actively considered. The scope for this energy source, however, is severely limited by the availability of suitable sites, so even in the long term it can make only a relatively small, though nevertheless useful, contribution to the world's energy supply.

A similar constraint applies to geothermal energy, which arises principally from the heat produced by natural radioactivity in the earth's crust. In some countries, for example New Zealand and Iceland, it has been extensively used for some time, but in a geologically stable country such as Britain even its ultimate potential is rather modest compared to our present energy demand.

Lastly, there is the daily inflow of energy from the sun, available to us either directly, or indirectly via the wind and the waves. Two endemic problems to be overcome, if we wish to use these sources, are their variability and their diffuseness, for their availability depends on the whims of the weather, and the energy is spread thinly over a large area. Man has been using some of these sources on a small scale for centuries. For example, there were some ten thousand or so windmills in use in Britain prior to the industrial revolution. But we have yet to master the technology of using them on a scale that is significant compared to our present level of energy consumption. What is more, at the present time the economics do not look too hopeful.

So the current situation with regard to these new sources of energy is that they offer exciting possibilities for the future, and therefore it would be wise to continue to investigate them. It would be very unwise, however, to rely on them, because at the present time we have no idea which if any of them will turn out to be practical, and we cannot say whether or not they will be able to provide us with significant amounts of energy at an acceptable price. Our present energy policy, therefore, in an era of depleting oil and gas, has to be based on a combination of energy conservation, coal and uranium.

What future for industrial society?

We come finally to what I believe to be the most important message of this chapter. We have seen how the severity of the energy problem obliges us to take more seriously our cultural mandate to act as responsible stewards of the natural world. We must conserve energy by using fuel more efficiently, we must press into service all the economic sources of energy that we can lay our hands on, and of course we must take care of the environment. The better we do all these things, the more we will ease the energy problem, and the longer we will postpone the energy crisis. However, here comes the rub. At best they can only *postpone* the problem; they cannot *solve* it. We might indeed postpone the problem long enough for it to be no longer *our* problem. We can pass it on to our descendants to find a solution, either in the next generation or perhaps even in the one after that, but sooner or later a solution must be found. No matter how efficiently we use energy, and however many new energy sources we learn to use, we cannot continue indefinitely down the road leading to a worldwide expanding industrial economy. The resources of the earth – in particular the energy resources – do not permit us to do so.

It is essential that the developing countries of the Third World be encouraged to strive to increase the material wealth of their peoples. So my message is addressed to those of us in the already developed industrial nations. I believe that the time has come for us to re-examine our life-styles. To do that we have to take a fundamental look at our industrial way of life. We must be prepared to challenge some of its basic concepts. It might well be a painful thing to do, because sub-consciously we tend to assume that industrial society is the ultimate stage in man's development. In fact, every age tends to assume that the stage of human development it has reached is the ultimate one. It is an assumption that has invariably proved wrong.

There is plenty of biblical guidance to help us in our quest. By way of example, let me take just two of the basic concepts of our industrial society and examine them in the light of Scripture. The first is the concept of sustained economic growth, the axiom which states that we should strive to make our economy expand year by year, and takes the size of the percentage increase achieved over the previous year as an indicator of our success. A covetous obsession with the acquisition of ever increasing amounts of material wealth is roundly condemned in Scripture. Think of the parable in Luke 12 about the man who pulled down his barns and built larger ones. Here was someone who according to our concept of economic growth had been enormously successful; so successful in fact that his barns could no longer contain all the material wealth he had produced, and he had to build larger ones to accommodate it all. Rather than congratulating him on his enterprise, however, God calls him a fool. It is a condemnation at variance with our assumed virtue of economic growth and the acquisition of yet more and more material wealth. It is a timely reminder to us that there is a lot more to life than just getting richer and richer, and that 'a man's life does not consist in the abundance of his possessions' (Luke 12:15).

Economic growth is an appropriate concept at certain times, under certain conditions and in certain places. For example, there are many countries in the world in which economic growth is needed – and needed on an heroic scale – to raise the living standards of their people to an acceptable level. Even in our own country some further growth may be necessary to enable us more easily to remove the inequalities and injustices of our society. There is no justification, however, for assuming that sustained economic growth is in the natural order of things; that it has universal validity for all times, in all conditions and in all places. To assume so is to believe in an illusion, and, because of the constraints imposed upon us by our finite world, it could well be a dangerous illusion. The time could come when sustained economic growth, at least as we have conventionally defined it in terms of increased material wealth, would be neither desirable nor achievable. We in our society may not have quite yet reached that point, but I believe that we are approaching it.

The second basic concept that I would like to examine is the attitude of our industrial society towards work. It has been called the 'protestant work ethic'; it asserts that work is a virtue and the harder we work the more virtuous we are and the greater our reward will be. There is nothing wrong with hard work, of course; indeed in a society seeking to raise its living standards to an acceptable level, the more of it the better. It is the attitude towards it in a society such as our own, particularly in the context of the ecological crisis which threatens us, that I wish to call in question.

There are two aspects to the problem. The first is that if we were all to work as hard as we could at creating wealth, with all the power that modern technology is increasingly putting at our elbow, we would find that before long we were stripping the earth of its energy resources, and most of its other material resources as well. We are entering an era in which we shall be able to supply all our legitimate demand for manufactured goods without all of us having to work a 40 hour week for most of our lives. This has serious political implications for future patterns of employment and a fair distribution of wealth; it also has more fundamental implications for our attitude towards work. The second aspect is the rather disturbing extent to which we regard our job as the justification of our lives; when asked what we 'are' we tend to reply in terms of the job we 'do'.

Let me remind you of the story of Mary and Martha at the end of Luke 10. Martha busied herself in the kitchen preparing a meal, while Mary spent the time sitting at the feet of Jesus listening to his words of wisdom. When Martha complained about the situation, it was she who received the mild rebuke and Mary who received the commendation. It is a story which makes strange reading to a generation such as our own brought up on the concept of the protestant work ethic. Perhaps, like me, you also have had to sit through many a convoluted sermon trying to explain it away. Is not the simple lesson to be learned from this story that we should not become so obsessed with our work – good though that may be – that we anaesthetise our minds to the more fundamental things of life; that we should regard work as a means to an end rather than an end in itself?

Pre-industrial man had to devote virtually every waking hour to back-breaking work merely to survive; even during his industrial phase he had to work long hours in order to keep up with the demand for the manufactured goods he had invented. The time spent working was regarded as the 'important' time; leisure pursuits and holidays were justified in terms of relaxation and re-creation that would make him better able to do his job. As we move into the automative age in which machines are becoming increasingly able to do our work for us, we are faced with perhaps a greater challenge – the challenge of leisure. It is the challenge of making constructive use of our time without the bulk of it being subject to the enforced discipline of routine work. It is the challenge, as traditional work takes a less dominant role, of thinking about the meaning and purpose of our lives.

There is a story told about a conversation between a philosopher and a labourer. The philosopher saw the labourer digging a ditch and asked him why he was doing it. The labourer replied; 'I dig the ditch to earn the money to buy the food to give me the strength to dig the ditch!' In the age of the mechanical digger, what then is there to give meaning to the labourer's life?

What is a post-industrial society?

The pressure on the world's material resources in general, and on energy resources in particular, arising from sustained and expanding industrial world developement, indicates quite clearly that advanced nations such as ours should be starting to think of other ways in which to develop. Britain was the first country to enter the industrial age; it would not seem inappropriate therefore that she should lead the way into the post-industrial age. The situation is not yet desperate, but all the signs are that it will become increasingly so; we have perhaps a generation or so in which to sort ourselves out. Unfortunately, nobody as yet has any definite idea as to what a post-industrial society is supposed to be like; the fact that we call it by that name rather than something more specific is a clear indication of that.

Many people have made suggestions, of course. Some authors[11] would have us believe that the future lies in what is effectively a return to a pre-industrial society – a vision which I personally find totally unattractive and unacceptable. Others[12] have painted at great length – one is tempted to say at inordinate length – a much more imaginative scenario for the future. In conclusion, therefore, perhaps I might be permitted a few speculations of my own.

One guess is that in the age we are about to enter, increasing numbers of us will earn our livings in what we now call the service industries rather than in the manufacturing industries. During our industrial phase such services were relegated to a secondary role, as something subservient to what we considered to be the real wealth creation activities of the manufacturing sector, or as optional extras to be paid for out of profits from that sector. Even today we still refer to the foreign currency earned by such service activities as banking, insurance and tourism – although they are now amongst the major earners of such currency – as 'invisible' imports. How big do they have to get before they become visible, one is tempted to ask?

Who is to say that a man who writes a poem has created less wealth than one who has made a motor car? The activity of the former certainly involves less consumption of raw materials than that of the latter; and this must surely be a feature of the post-industrial age, namely that it will impose a lower demand on the world's energy and other material resources. One can also hope that a society whose main economic activity is in service rather than manufacture will grow to be a more caring society.

Another guess is that structured work as we now know it will play a less dominant role in our lives than it does at present. The political problems with which such a transition faces us are truly enormous, and we have barely begun to think how to solve them. Will it mean a shorter working week? Longer holidays? Earlier retirement? Some form of work sharing? How will people be able to acquire an adequate income if they spend less time in paid employment? Provided that we can solve these problems, however, the prospect of a more leisured society is an attractive one – not to idle our time away in aimless pastimes, but rather to have the opportunity to do all the things we have always wanted to do if only we did not have to spend so much of each day earning our living.

Of course the future may not be like that at all; only time will tell. One thing is certain, however: because of the constraints imposed upon us by the material resources of one finite world, the future cannot be a mere perpetuation of the present.

1 K. J. Walker, 'Materials consumption; implications in a full industrialised world', Resources Policy (Dec. 1979).
2 M. King Hubbert, *Energy Resources*, Washington DC National Academy of Sciences (1962).

3 Don Headley, *World Energy: the Facts and the Future* (Euromonitor Publications, 1981).
4 P. Aggaswamy et al, *Estimates of Risks Associated with Dam Failure* (UCLA – ENG – 7423, 1974).
5 J. Gribbin and J. Tinker, *Carbon Dioxide, the Climate and Man* (Earthscan, London, 1981).
6 *The Environmental Impact of Nuclear Power* (BNES, 1981).
7 I. M. Blair, *The Taming of the Atom* (Adam Hilger, Ltd., 1982).
8 R. A. D. Ferguson, *Comparative Risks of Electricity Generating Fuel Systems in the* UK (Peter Peregrinus, Ltd., 1981).
9 Gerald Leach, *A Low Energy Strategy for the United Kingdom* (Science Reviews Ltd., 1979).
10 L. G. Brookes, 'Review of the Leach Report', ATOM UKAEA (March 1979).
11 e.g. 'Blueprint for Survival', *The Ecologist*, (Jan 1972).
12 e.g. Alvin Toffler in *Future Shock* (Pan Books, 1971) and *Third Wave* (Collins, 1980).

As well as the above references, the interested reader may find the following works of value:

I. M. Blair, B. Jones and A. Van Horn, ed., *Aspects of Energy Conversion* (Pergammon Press, 1976).
Shaping Tomorrow, (Methodist Home Missions Division, 1981).

5 The New Technology: the Human Debate

Sir Fred Catherwood
(Member of the European Parliament)

Three years ago Clive Jenkins wrote a book entitled *The Collapse of Work*[1] and, knowing that I would disagree, sent me a copy. The centre-piece was the statement that the micro-processor 'is a technology, the main attribute of which increases productivity rather than stimulating production'. This pessimistic view follows a traditional attitude to inventions throughout the course of the industrial revolution, and it is easy to see why. Everyone can see the jobs which will be made obsolete, but no-one knows enough about the invention itself to see what jobs it is likely to create.

So, despite the enormous increase in employment which has gone hand in hand with the industrial revolution of the last 200 years, and despite the explosion of innovation and wealth in the last thirty years, the public mood is one of the deepest pessimism.

Christian Attitudes and Recent Trends
Christians must be in favour of full employment, for all that we believe points to it. Our love for our neighbour demands that while he is in need, we should work to supply his needs. It is absurd that while there are slums, building workers should be unemployed, and that while there is want – in our own country or elsewhere – those who could supply the want should be laid off. We can understand why these things happen, but we must try to put right what has gone wrong and not try to rationalise the perversity into some kind of sacred economic system.

The Christian should also be in favour of innovation. The parables of the talents and the pounds, found in Matthew 25 and Luke 19, tell us to multiply our talents. We should not be content with passing on no more than we have been given. If we have five talents, we should create five more, if two, then two more. The one unforgivable sin is to bury our talent. So the professional person must add to the knowledge passed on to him, he must take the state of the art to new levels; the skilled worker must find better ways of doing things; and the unskilled must acquire whatever skills he can.

The scientific method itself is based on a Christian view of the universe. We believe in one God the Creator; so we believe in unified laws of nature. Wherever and whenever we study them, the laws of nature will be the same. We believe in a God of order, who made everything in an orderly manner, after its kind; so the laws of nature will be orderly, capable of classification. We believe in a rational God, who gives mankind reasons with his 'maker's instructions', who argues cause and effect, so that every action will have a reaction. Therefore we believe in a rational universe, in which the process of cause and effect can be worked out into a rational system of knowledge. We believe in the truth of God's promise that the universe will be stable until the end of time, that its laws will therefore be the same tomorrow and the day after as they are today. None of these four propositions can be proved by the scientific method; they are the pillars on which the method rests, the reason why it emerged where and when it did. But they belong to the background of Christian thinking, that the material world was given to man in trust; it was not his own to use or abuse as he wished, but was there in divine providence 'for the relief of man's estate'. So the motive for scientific research is the study of 'the book of God's works', in order to discover the provisions he has made for mankind. It is this motive which will drive the Christian on and make him extremely reluctant to slow down the pace of scientific discovery.

But the Christian will, for the same reason, want to make sure that scientific research is benign, that it is to create and not to destroy, that it is to pass on a better earth to future generations and not to create deserts and dustbowls through greed in one generation. So economic growth must be based on genuine improvements in technology, which create the growth from existing resources and leave succeeding generations with a greater potential than we ourselves inherited.

Christians believe that man was made in the image of God the Creator and that, despite his fall through rebellion against God, we all still have this image of God in us, this feeling of fulfilment in creative work, in making something new which bears our own unique imprint. We are not creatures just of habit, following purely animal instincts. We want, at least, to be contributing; and if we are not wanted, if we are thrown out of work and unable to contribute, then we feel depressed and frustrated.

In looking at the result of new inventions on the level of employment, therefore, the Christian will want to balance the need for innovation with the need to preserve employment. Both are important.

What is remarkable is that the exceptional period of innovation since the second world war has also been a period of exceptional growth in employment. Despite the population growth and a great increase in the number of women at work, unemployment has, until the last few years, been much lower than it was between the wars. So the record so far does not show that innovation creates unemployment. Indeed, those countries with the greatest investment in innovation – Sweden, Switzerland, Germany and Japan – have had the lowest rates of unemployment, while those with the lowest rates of investment in innovation – the USA and the UK – have had the highest rates of unemployment. And the highest unemployment of all has been in the most backward countries.

It is fascinating to thumb through the employment statistics in Britain over several decades and to note the tremendous changes in employment patterns that there have been. For instance, the entire category of domestic servants has been wiped out, while a new industry, not in the statistics in the 20s and 30s, ladies' hairdressing, has sprung up. No central planning organisation could have engineered the change, and no Clive Jenkins could have forecast it, but it happened. And it was technology which helped it happen: the vacuum cleaner, the washing machine, the tumble drier and central heating all conspired towards the demise of the domestic servant, while more cheap gadgetry allowed ladies' hairdressing salons to appear in every High Street.

Transport provides another example. When, in the 1920s, technology produced reliable public road transport, it undercut the railways by 50 per cent, and there was a public outcry from that bastion of employment. Although employment in railways has continued to go down, employment in total surface transport by road and rail has vastly increased. The same is true of the new competition between air and surface transport. An enlarged Stansted Airport is forecast to employ 20,000 to 50,000 people. To those of us who first flew as passengers in the 1940s, when a provincial airport would scarcely have employed more than 100 people and everything was delightfully casual, the idea of an airport employing 20,000, let alone 50,000, would have seemed incredible. The vast increase has been brought about not by a shift from surface transport to air, but because the arrival of the jet in the 1960s made long distance travel so comparatively cheap, quick and reliable that it attracted a new class of traveller: the package tourists. These now outnumber the regular business traveller by about three to one. But the business travellers have increased enormously in number as well, as international trade has expanded, not only because tariffs have lowered, but also because salesmen and engineers are now able to travel swiftly and easily to find customers and to service them.

The Advent of the Micro-chip

But, Clive Jenkins would say, the micro-chip is an entirely different new technology. He and the other 'pessimists' argue that the micro-processor is a genuinely revolutionary device, and that the threat (never realised) of unemployment from computers in the 1950s, will now be realised in the 1980s. He draws attention to a report by the Advisory Council on Applied Research and Development written in September 1978 on semi-conductor technology.[2] The report said that first, the micro-chip both extends and displaces a wide range of intuitive skills; secondly, it is all-pervasive; thirdly, it is still advancing rapidly; fourthly, it is very cheap and getting cheaper; fifthly, it is abundantly available from international sources; and sixthly, it has exceptional reliability. Clive Jenkins infers from this that vast numbers of jobs will disappear.

But there is an optimists' side to the debate as well. These argue that labour-saving technology is nothing new and, as I have begun to explain, has never increased unemployment in the long term. The optimists' view point is that micro-processors will create new wealth, which will be spent on new products and services, which in turn will create new jobs. The Department of Employment, in its report on the manpower implications of micro-electronic technology, produced in 1979[3], argues this case coherently. This report cannot accept the 'gloomier view' which, it says, is 'hard to square with the fact that Western industrialised countries have experienced an almost continuous period since 1945 of both rapid technological change and increased employment'.[4]

Taking the longer view, it says, 'the evidence from the economic history of the entire industrial age is that technological change has been beneficial to aggregate employment'.[5] In its conclusions it states: 'the economic factors leading to employment shift, as a result of technological change, are complex and inevitably involve both job-displacing and compensatory job-creating mechanisms . . . However, past empirical works suggest that, in the long run, technological change has been beneficial to both output and employment'.[6]

Finally, the DOE Report points out that we are a trading country in a competitive world: 'If British industry fails to adopt new technology at least as fast as its overseas competitors, it will lose competitiveness, and demand for its produce will fall, with serious effect on employment levels.'[7]

Another excellent summary of the arguments is to be found in *The Microelectronics Revolution* edited by Tom Forester. It gives both the pessimistic and the optimistic arguments. Philip Sadler, summarising both points of view, says, 'The threat to employment opportunities from the new technology in Europe may be in danger of being over-emphasised. I believe that the greater danger is posed by increasing industrialisation in other (less developed) parts of the world, and that technology is useful in answering this threat,'[8] Despite these reports, it has become accepted wisdom that the micro-chip destroys jobs without creating enough others. We ought therefore to look more closely at exactly what a micro-chip is and what it does.

A micro-chip is not magic. It is a complex of circuits on a tiny chip of silicon: 'a computer on a chip' is one way of defining it. Since it is an incredibly powerful and very small computer, we can look at examples of what computers have done in industry.

My first example is a small aluminium plant in the Highlands of Scotland which did not have enough water in its catchment area to keep its turbo-generators running at full capacity all the year. In order to get the optimum production from the shortlife carbon boxes in which aluminium is melted, it needed to have the best possible forecast of the water flow from the catchment area. So it fed into the computer the following information: the rainfall from the water gauges, the rainfall pattern in the Highlands for the last eighty years, the time the water took to drain off the tops and into the river, and the expected life of the smelting boxes. The computer then gave the management the optimum relationship between the rainfall pattern and their smelting programme. The result was to use as nearly as possible all the energy available from the water power, giving a higher output from existing investment.

There were incidental hazards. The owners of the neighbouring deer forest, believing that employees of the smelter were poaching their deer, filled their rainwater gauges up to the brim in the hope that that would give the computer the hiccoughs.

My second example is a Midlands tube plant where the computer sorts out daily orders in the plant, allocates them to the machines which can handle them, compares them with existing orders on those machines, and, taking into account the capacity of each machine, puts the orders on the machine in an optimum production run in order to achieve minimal tool changes and the lowest down time.

The result of this systemisation is to enable the plant to run with lower stocks of raw material, shorter delivery dates, more reliable delivery times and lower running costs. It produces a better performance on the machinery available, giving a much higher potential output from the plant.

The considered view of most companies today is that the computer enables them to handle their business from the production process through to distribution much more precisely, with less waste and much better performance, and that on the whole it is more likely to add jobs, as the companies expand to take up the potential created by the computer, than it is to lose jobs. And of course they do not take into account in their job calculation the work of the computer company employees and all the software jobs, the detailed process of telling the machine what to do in every conceivable event, which go with the installation of a computer.

The on-line computer in the steel mill was a big traditional machine, in a room beside the rolling mill. But the break-through made by the micro-processor, which is the reduction of the computer's brain to a tiny silicon chip, is that it enables the on-line computer to become a part of the machinery itself. So it is not just the rolling mill operator who hands over to a computer, but the operator of almost any kind of machinery and even the pilot of an aircraft. For just as the big computer enables the rolling mill to react to the size, shape and temperature of the metal and make an adjustment of the controls to an optimum pitch which the human operator could not calculate so precisely, so the relatively cheap micro-processor can operate on all kinds of machinery with a speed and delicacy of adjustment and a level of consistency which the human eye and hand simply cannot match. And yet even here the main benefit of the micro-chip is in achieving a consistency of performance in the product and in getting a faster through-put. If the rate of demand is high enough, as it is for instance for a Japanese car assembly, then the result is higher output and not lower employment.

If we move from the production line to aircraft, we find that the micro-processor, with its capacity to make instant adjustments to the aircraft's instruments and configuration, in order to keep it on a pre-determined flight path or glide path for landing, is wholly in the interests of safety, since passenger aircraft will always need a pilot. We all know the old joke about the recorded cockpit announcement to passengers that they had been the first unmanned takeoff. The recorded voice ending the announcement said 'and now we wish you a good flight . . . a good flight . . . a good flight . . . a good flight. . . . '

The micro-chip has revolutionised the watch industry, but we still wear watches – and much more accurate ones. It has produced an entirely new pocket calculator industry, and in the medical world a new industry for the production of brain and body scanners which are a breakthrough in the early diagnosis and the precise locations of cancers. We must all know of a friend or relative who would not have died if they had been given a scan in time.

So we cannot say that the micro-processor will inevitably destroy jobs. If the economic atmosphere were different today, if there were high economic growth, less de-industrialisation, and a growing public sector, then the micro-technology revolution would no doubt be welcomed. Some certainly would lose their jobs, but their capacity to find another job would be great in an expanding economy which was spending increasing sums, incidentally, on high technology training.

The difficulty now is that two phenomena have merged. The micro-processor revolution has arrived at the same time as a world recession brought on by the huge rise in the price of oil and the resulting Arab dollar surpluses which have de-stabilised the world economies since 1973. This recession has been exacerbated in the United Kingdon by a series of factors: a serious lack of competitiveness, due mainly to a much lower rate of innovative investment; rapid de-industrialisation (the movement of employment from industry to services) which is a result of greater productivity, though this has no connection with the micro-chip; and slashing cuts in public expenditure brought on by the need to cut inflation. This could hardly be a worse climate for the micro-processor revolution, and it is hardly surprising that the 'pessimists' were, at least until recently, hogging the debate.

The main price the world is paying for the recession is mass unemployment, 3 million in the United Kingdom, 10 million in the European Community; and these figures look like rising. This is not the place to argue about the politics of allowing unemployment to stay at its present levels. The point is that large numbers of people look like being unemployed *whether or not* we allow the micro-processor revolution to take place. The major difference is that if we do not allow it to take place, then, if and when the economic atmosphere changes for the better, we will have been left behind, by both Japan and the USA, and by our partners in Europe.

My argument is then not only that we need to pursue the revolution in order to keep up with our competitors, but also because of my belief in the micro-processor's ability to create new jobs and in its ability to create wealth to train for other high technology skills those whom it makes redundant.

Small is Beautiful

The micro-chip of course has already created new jobs in high technology: those who research, service and run the new industry. But I accept that these will not provide jobs for those made redundant by the technology. What about the mass of the working population, those whom Clive Jenkins represents? Of course there will be a huge expansion in the service industries and in education. Beyond that we can only speculate. It is quite possible that the whole industrial scene with big mass production plants in the pattern set by Henry Ford may disappear. For the computer does not have to be in the plant. The computer is only in the plant because the plant was there in the first place. And the plant, with its miles of production line all under one roof, was there because management needed to see and supervise everything that was going on. But the more the computer governs the production flow, the less necessary it is to have the production flow in one place. And the more reliable the robotics become, the less necessary it is to supervise the operator. We all know about the vast volume production of Japanese cars. The application of robotics – welding machines, for instance, controlled by micro-processors – needs a small number of people employed in the final production line. I once visited two production lines of Honda, one for motor cycles and one for cars, employing between them only 3,000 people. But the production line depended on a vast sub-contracting industry, and this was not based on a few big suppliers but on thousands of very small ones. Indeed, part of the objection of the European car industry to the Japanese competition is the assumption that, because there are so many small suppliers, these must be employing sweated labour. That is only because we associate small suppliers with old pre-mass production workshops. But there is no real reason why the small supplier should be any less well equipped than the big one.

And when we look at the statistics of industrial disputes, we find that the very small shopfloor has practically no time lost through disputes. Time lost grows with the size of the shopfloor. It becomes noticeable on plants with 500 employees, while the curve rises steeply with 1,000 and over, and more steeply still in the really big plants of 5,000 and above. An escape from the formal structured world of the huge plant with 5,000 employees, distant management, and feelings of the emptiness and futility of it all, is to find work in the so called 'black' economy. For example, your plumber, who is miraculously free in the evenings, asks you for cash for the work he has just done, – and then the following morning you catch sight of him walking into your local factory gates. People want this extra work, not just because they do not like to pay tax, but because it gives them greater independence and less regimentation. Above all, it takes them away from the feeling that they are only a small cog in a large machine. Women especially find it easier to work at home, and the whole problem of 'latchkey kids' could be overcome if a woman was able to do her work at home in her own time, instead of being forced to work on a shift in a factory.

If man, made in the image of God with a creative spirit, is made to work as part of a machine, as if he were no more than a fractional horse-power engine, with a cheap and slightly unreliable control mechanism, his nature will rebel against it. In the insistence of organised labour that it will not be treated as part of the production process, and its further insistence every now and again on putting a very human spoke in the well-oiled production machine, we have seen an obstinate expression of humanity. The bigger the place of work, the more powerful this insistence becomes. If the micro-chip enables us to reorganise our production from the huge impersonal production line where the man is part of the machine, into a smaller, more independent, production unit, where the man does what only a man can do, it will have gone a long way towards the humanisation of industry.

I suppose I have walked round as many shopfloors as most people. In doing to, I have found a remarkable difference between the big plants where the boss does not know the worker and the small ones where everyone knows everyone else. In the former there is a sense of alienation. In many you could cut the atmosphere with a knife. In the latter, where communication is a natural part of human life, the plant is more like an extended family.

When I was Chairman of the British Overseas Trade Board, and we ran 'export year' with the help of the shopfloor, I remember the story of one large plant in the North of England. In a fit of export enthusiasm and togetherness the management asked the workers how to overcome a production bottleneck on a particularly difficult machine. The workers told them. 'Why ever didn't you tell us this before?' asked the management. 'You never asked us before,' the workers replied.

It is not only true that 'small is beautiful' and practical, but I believe that, with the micro-chip, it can also create jobs better than the big plant with all its built-in inflexibility. The use of the micro-chip in robotics may do away with the manned production line and with the use of creative human beings as if they were no more than production line levers. But it will also enable production to be decentralised into very small units, both by its capacity to organise production wherever the production units are located and by its capacity to programme machines to produce without heavy technical supervision. So, in a country with fairly concentrated population and good communications, production can leave the giant works employing 8,000 and be dispersed to tiny companies working in small industrial estates in each village.

Cottage industry is back again – but this time subject to the Factory Acts.

In Cambridgeshire, where I live and which I represent in the European Parliament, there is a higher than average level of employment. It is based, with few exceptions, on very small companies on small trading estates in small towns like St Ives and St Neots, or villages like Melbourn, where I first acquired a micro-chip. These little companies compete internationally and win the Queen's Award for Exports and for Technology. They are perhaps more heavily into electronics than anything else, and the presence nearby of the University and its research is obviously a help. But what has been done in Cambridgeshire can be and is being done elsewhere.

Why do smaller firms offer better job prospects than the big company? First, they are nearer to, and usually more responsible to, the market. For the customer, it's like leaving your car in a small garage where you can talk to the mechanic who is fixing it. You know him and he knows you. Your car does not reappear in the hands of a receptionist who has no idea what has been going on. From the company's point of view, everyone in the plant knows what the customer needs, why changes need to be made, and why the company has to adapt in order to keep its customers. Walking round the small plant, everyone can tell you the story.

In the big plant there is a gap of distrust between management and workers, and into this gap comes the necessary machinery of consultation, either organised into a trades union structure or set up for the purpose. But, like all big organisations, it tends to become formal. A case can be made and understood, but not accepted, for fear of creating a precedent. Employees know that higher wages will create redundancies, but they just hope that they do not draw the short straw. The case of adopting new working methods takes longer. Sometimes it fails completely. The imposition of standards is a continual battle. A minority of poor workers ride on the backs of the rest

138

and, in the formal atmosphere of labour relations, the Union feels that it must protect them for fear that hardly earned rights are abused.

By contrast, in the small company, everyone feels that they are in it together and that their jobs depend on their own performance. So they are much more flexible and adaptable, and (because they are nearer to the market) more capable of surviving and of expanding. Of course, with present legislation, which favours oligopoly and the take-over of small companies by large, and which discourages joint marketing by small companies, it is the survival of the fattest and not of the fittest. To make the world safe for the most effective form of business, we need a decisive change in the legal bias.

I once asked a small exporter why he did not double his production and take on another 200 workers. He was in an area of high unemployment. His reply was that he knew, and could work with, the 200 he had now. If he doubled his output and workforce, there was a risk that he would not be as fortunate. If all went well, he would be taxed on the extra profits he took out of the business at 98%. If he left them in the business, Capital Transfer Tax would eventually remove them. If, on the other hand, he sold out to a conglomerate, he would make a fortune. Since then the tax laws have changed.

At the very smallest size, the micro-chip will enable many more people to work for themselves or in family units. It will make it far easier for a family business to keep track of what is happening. A fairly cheap computer is now all that is needed to keep the accounts, to show what products pay and what do not, and to give guidelines which will keep the bank account in the black. In the world of big business, wage costs are not flexible. You either get the full wage or the sack. There is little in between except short-time working – and that does not reduce unit costs. The family business, on the other hand, is able to set the lean months off against the good months and to decide whether to keep going or not.

In our industrial society, most people have had to find work in an organisation. The organisation has had tax and pension privileges which the individual has not had. But it is not part of the organisation's duties to create work. It is its duty to minimise costs, to find customers, to pay taxes and dividends – but not to find jobs. And it is not the state's duty to provide jobs either. It, too, has to work within its tax revenue and borrowing power. So if the technological revolution makes it possible for people to set up in business for themselves, it restores to society the flexibility we lost when mass production took over from the crafts. If the micro-chip provides governors on machines which look after the technical specification of the product, and data processsing which looks after the chores of business management, then a lot more people will be freed from the necessity of going out cap in hand to look for employment in a big organisation. Instead, they will be free to do their own thing, to create their own business, and even to use the computer to design their own products.

The Effects of Technical Innovation.

You may say, of course, that this is all very well for those who have the skill to do it, but what of the semi-skilled, and what of those who have no skill at all?

We have to remember that there was a time when most of the country was unskilled. The man of the world might have thought they they were not worth educating. But we now have universal education. What we lack is training in the skills. We are far behind countries like Germany. We cannot honestly say that all those who are not skilled now, never can be. For there is still much potential in our national work force waiting to be developed. I talked a short time ago to Singapore's leading banker. His grandfather had been a coolie. No doubt the colonial powers of the day thought that this was all that his family were good for. They were wrong! Insofar as there will always be some who cannot acquire skills, they will be carried by the economic growth engendered by those who can, though the Christian will always want to make work more creative and minimise the number of jobs which are no more than a chore.

Next, we have to look at the wider effects of technical innovation. Those who want to hold back the advance of inventiveness and technology seem to have no conception of the needs of the wider world in which we live. The population of the world is forecast to expand from 4,000 million to over 6,000 million by the end of century. With widespread under-nourishment in the world as it is, we desperately need to expand food production to keep up with the advancing population, and that in turn needs an increase both in energy output and in methods of conservation. For if we are not to create deserts and dustbowls beyond the end of the century, then we need vastly to improve our technical capacity to increase output without using up scarce and non-renewable resources. In all the debate about world hunger and in the north-south dialogue, we tend to overlook the enormous dependence of the poverty-stricken parts of the world on the pace and development of the great production machine of the industrial democracies and the need to adapt it to minimise its use of oil and scarce materials.

And if we look at the reasons for the slow-down of that machine, they have very little to do with the pace of inventiveness, and everything to do with the sluggish application of inventions to new products and new plants to make them.

Even when demand has been fairly constant, there are all kinds of opposition to the application of new inventions.

First, innovation may create new jobs but it certainly upsets employment patterns, and it is the existing employment patterns which are highly organised politically while the potentially new industries are not. So every innovation comes as a threat to jobs in particular industries represented by particular employers' organisations and trade unions, and to plants in particular towns represented by

141

particular members of parliament. The innovation may produce twice as much work, and may be absolutely essential to the economic growth of the country and the development of the Third World, but those who would eventually benefit are not organised to express their views. So we hear all about the risk, whereas the opportunity is never expressed with the same vehemence or political clout.

Secondly, there is human inertia. We may be inventive, but when it comes to risking our jobs or our money, or throwing away all our hard-won experience to learn something entirely new, then we become resistant. So trade unions, managements, boards of directors and shareholders all combine to look at change with great doubt and anxiety.

But thirdly, and perhaps most important, there is natural and powerful resistance in a stagnant economy when change leads inevitably to redundancy and unemployment. I am an unrepentant believer in economic growth, not least because it minimises the social problems of technological innovation. There is nothing too upsetting about changing jobs. People do it all the time. In a lifetime, we all get accustomed to doing different kinds of work. I have certainly practised what I preach. But redundancy, when there is nowhere to go but the dole queue, is another matter. In a highly industrialised society, the unemployed are not just worse off; they are stateless and functionless. They do not belong. No-one wants them. And so understandably they resist, as long as they can, the changes which make them redundant.

From the 1940s to the 1970s, the industrial nations of the world managed a remarkable and unprecedented burst of economic growth. It was based on the monetary cooperation set up under the Bretton Woods agreement institutionalised in the World Bank, and on the lowering of trade barriers under the General Agreement on Tariffs and Trade (GATT). All was monitored by the Organisation for Economic Cooperation and Development. And it was certainly fuelled by apparently limitless sources of cheap energy, though a steady rise in energy costs could have been taken in its stride.

Under this dynamic group of international institutions, it paid business to innovate and to invest in new products and new processes. The policy of full employment encouraged employees to accept change and the higher rewards which usually went with new work. As old plants and obsolete processes were closed down, new ones took their place. The problems were minimal.

But after 30 years people began to take progress for granted. A wealthier society left some of the old virtues of give and take behind, became more materialistic, more demanding, insisting on rights and forgetting that we cannot have rights without corresponding duties. The symptom was inflation, which first destabilised the relationship between currencies, and then imposed higher and higher costs on the producers of fuel, food and raw materials, until the oil producers formed a cartel and struck back with two immense price rises in 1973 and 1979. Now the industrialised world is desperately trying to restore the foundations, while high and rising unemployment gives urgency to the task. I have spent more time on this issue lately in the European Parliament than on anything else!

In the short run, we can get rid of high unemployment only by putting right what has gone wrong in the world's economic system. I believe that the European Community is now big enough to take over from America the job of economic recovery, and I hope that the European Parliament will shortly produce concrete proposals.

In the medium term, we have to decide whether the European Community and our trading partners in Western Europe can continue to offer open markets to the newly industrialised countries of East Asia without reciprocal access to their markets. If – hopefully – we gain access, we will not be threatened (as we have been) with loss of industries for which there is no obvious replacement. If – unhappily – we cannot gain access, then we must decide whether we can and should protect ourselves, so that full employment is not threatened. This case is put by Wolfgand Hager in a compelling article in the Summer 1982 number of *International Affairs*.[9]

I am myself convinced that Christians who believe that the natural world was given to man in trust and for his benefit have to put their mind and will to rediscovering a framework for economic development. But, since we are only trustees for life of natural resources, such a framework must not, this time, use up scarce non-renewable resources, but instead, use technology to help us both save energy and create new sources. It must pay a fair price to the primary producers of the Third World.

It must also be based on a much more stable relation between productivity and wages, and on a fair share in decision-making by the wage-earner, whose collective financial stake is usually much higher than that of the owner and banker.

It is not clear yet whether the vested interests of capital and labour are ready to give up defensive positions. Nor is it clear whether the Protestant ethic, which gave us the scientific method and the idea of economic development, has been so heavily undermined that defensive attitudes of work-sharing, shorter hours and early retirement can be overcome. The Third World depends on its being overcome. My own feeling is that the next expansion, when it comes, will be through smaller, more personal working groups. The demise of the giant plant and the rise of the black economy point that way. A great deal of innovation in new technology like electronics is going on in very small companies, who take their own risks and go their own way, untrammelled by a distant head office or the restrictions imposed by over-weighty unions. This is how I see the emergence of job-creating technology. It will not come with a few big bangs from a big government handout for a giant car plant, but by a sustained barrage from small guns on a very wide front.

1 Clive Jenkins and Barrie Sherman, *The Collapse of Work*, (Eyre Methuen, 1979).
2 Advisory Council for Applied Research and Development, *The Application of Semi-Conductor Technology*, (September 1978).
3 Department of Employment Study Group, 'The Manpower Implications of Micro-Electronic Technology', (1979).
4 Ibid. p. 7.
5 Ibid. p. 9.
6 Ibid. p. 106.
7 Ibid.
8 Sadler, P. 'Welcome Back to the Automation Debate', in Tom Forester (ed) *The Microelectronics Revolution* (Basil Blackwell – Oxford, 1980).
9 Wolfgang Hager, 'Protectionism and Autonomy: How to preserve free trade in Europe', *International Affairs*, Vol. 58, No. 3, (Summer 1982).

6 Authority and Democracy: the Political Debate

Professor Martin Harrison
(*Professor and Head of Department of Politics,
University of Keele*)

Dark though the futurologist's glass must often be, we can look towards the year 2000 with two certainties. First, that the agenda of politics will be crowded, and that many of the issues will be matters on which Christian voices can and should be heard. Secondly, that then as now the basic problems of man-in-society will find no final resolution in political ideologies or action. If there seems to be a dissonance between these two assertions, it is apparent rather than real. For 'state', 'government' and 'politics' are all part of God's ordering of things for man (Rom. 13.1). Like any of his gifts they can be abused, but they are also channels through which Christians may bear witness to the truth, not least by giving practical expression to their love and compassion for their fellow men and women: 'Anything you did for one of my brothers here, however humble, you did for me' (Mat. 25.40). And yet, as Haddon Willmer so gently puts it, 'The state is always in some measure a failure'[1]. Again, 'There is a great gulf between what the church knows is true and what is possible for the world.'[2] Or, in the timeless words of Augustine, 'True justice is not to be found, except in that republic whose foundation and ruler is Christ' – a Kingdom which is not of this world.

Much the same comments can be applied to almost any form of Christian social involvement. Yet many Christians seem to find them curiously more bothersome where politics is involved. Within the recognition that every human activity falls painfully short of divine perfection, politics is so often treated as peculiarly corrupt compared with (say) marriage guidance or prison visiting. Peter Hinchliff, an Anglican specialist in relations between Church and state, surely voiced a widely held view in commenting that 'ordinary decent behaviour, let alone the over-riding claim of Christ upon the Christian, is not compatible with public life', and in concluding that 'society as a whole has come to the conclusion that it is impossible to apply normal moral standards to the affairs of politics.'[3]

This is not the place for either a defence of politics against easy calumny or a lengthy reflection on the theology of the state. Briefly, however, I am not persuaded by those venerable strands of Christian social theory that tend to identify the 'earthly city' with the 'city of Cain', or which see government as merely God's remedy for human disorder resulting from the fall. Such traditions die hard. Even as sociologically aware an advocate of Christian political involvement as Alan Storkey can badly assert that 'the state was instituted because of sin.'[4] This is far too audacious a conclusion to draw from either the early appearance of judges in Israel or from passages like Peter's reminder that rulers are 'sent by God to punish those who do wrong and to praise those who do right' (1 Pet. 2.14). This text is not a statement about the origins of government; besides it intimates that governments have wider functions than coping with wrongdoing. Such interpretations encourage too negative and restrictive an idea of government. To cut cavalierly through a very tangled theological thicket, I stand with those who believe that the origins of government and politics are more profitably traced back to the diversity of creation, with all that implies for social organisation, than to the fall.

Obviously, punishing wrongdoing and dealing with the consequences of sin – the victims of crime and war, of family breakdown, of economic exploitation, and much else besides – are significant government activities. But even a morally perfect social order, unless it was credited with perfect knowledge and unlimited abundance, would still need government to turn its diversity into effective collective action. Even in our far from perfect societies, vast tracts of political activity have no plausible origin in 'sin'. And so it has ever been. For example, Lucy Mair's description of traditional African government shows the elders of the Karamojong of Uganda regulating the movement of cattle, and the council of elders of the Nandi people of Kenya dealing with 'disasters such as drought, invasion of locusts and diseases of cattle' as well as with the 'redress of wrongs'.[5]

Whatever the origins of government, and however great the distaste of some Christians for the seamier facets of politicking, they must never forget that government is not a mere necessary evil; it is divinely ordained and actively commended to us (1 Pet. 2.14; Rom. 13.1–6). As Bonhoeffer put it, albeit a trifle awkwardly, 'One need only hold out something to be God-willed and God-created for it to be vindicated for ever.'[6] For all their failings, government and politics are to be celebrated, supported and put to constructive use. If their flaws are more cruelly public than those of other forms of social action, neither empirically nor theologically have we the right to consider them more real or more profound.

With such a climate of discussion, it is scarcely surprising that some Christians have been so fearful of being defiled by the pitch of politics, or of succumbing to 'social gospelling', that they have withdrawn into a prudent pietism. Others have drifted to a position where a veneer of religiosity overlays an unthinking if well-meaning set of liberal-democratic attitudes to the point where any distinctive Christian identity is extinguished. In short, in a world of widespread injustice, much of it institutionalised,[7] Christians are too often torn between being on the one hand 'Pharisees' or 'Levites' passing all this by on the other side, or on the other wishy-washy Laodiceans – when they should really be thinking in terms of the

PRUDENT PIETISM
SOCIAL GOSPELING

challenging affirmations of the Word of God to man. That Word is 'living and active, sharper than any two-edged sword, piercing to the division of soul and spirit, of joints and marrow, and discerning the thoughts and intentions of the heart' (Heb. 4.12, 13).

Government, then, is ordained under the sovereignty of God (Dan. 4.18; also Exod.15; Exod.18; Ps.2; Acts 4.23–31).[8] Its authority comes from him. As Jesus told Pilate, 'You would have no authority at all over me . . . if it had not been granted you from above' (John 19.11). Power may be used for good or evil, but whether they acknowledge him or not, rulers are God's servants (Rom. 13.4), subject to his law (Deut. 17.18–20) and to his judgment (Acts 12.21; Col. 4.1; Ps. 2.11–12). They are owed obedience (Rom. 1.35), loyalty (Titus 3.1–8), honour (1 Pet. 2.17) and constant intercession (1 Tim. 2.1–2).[9] Yet as the first duty of Christians is to God rather than man, 'the Christian can never yield an unqualified submission to any secular authority.'[10] The task of Christians is clearly to work for righteousness wherever they find themselves. Or as Bishop Henson, again, put it, Christianity cannot be placed 'in the category of private opinion, which a man may cherish but by which he must not seriously guide his civil behaviour.'[11] The 'critical involvement' to which Christian citizens are called is far from easy, but then working through the implications of being 'in the world but not of the world' rarely is.

Big Government – Past and Future

To look forward, we must first look back. Historians will differ about the point from which we should date the expansion of the concerns of government. That it reaches back into the last century can scarcely be challenged. For some this growth has become almost a moral problem in itself. The 1970s in particular saw a vogue for the view that 'small is beautiful'. There may indeed be many collective goods that are best achieved through small-scale endeavour. And in matters of political organisation we would be hard put to produce scriptural warrant for a belief that 'God is on the side of the big battalions'. Nevertheless, as a systematic approach to social action in modern society, the stress on smallness is little better than sentimental utopianism. More fashionably, free-market prophets like Professors Hayek and Friedman have argued as if we have been sliding towards serfdom ever since the days of that dangerous interventionist Shaftesbury. Some of the more dogmatic members of this school suggest that as much as two-thirds of public expenditure could be eliminated by 2000 AD. If such talk is meant as anything more than a polemical *jeu d'esprit*, consider the reality of the resulting minimalist state. Outside the black comedy of Catch 22, even the most zealous privatisers hesitate to contract defence out to the highest bidder. In anything like the present international climate – which has to be reckoned with if in no sense 'accepted' – the wholesale transfer of other functions from government to the free market would produce a garrison state. How could this possibly claim the affection and support of its people? How, for that matter, can one envisage the interplay of great industrial and commercial institutions, trade unions and media conglomerates, barely restrained by a vestigial government, leading to justice, welfare and the protection of the weak? (And surely concern for justice in its broadest and most searching senses is one of the most recurrent strands in biblical social teaching right from the Genesis account of Cain's dealings with Abel).

It would be foolish to pretend that we can foresee whether the scope of government and politics will tend, overall, to shrink or expand over the next generation. But one of our few political certainties about the year 2000 is that 'big government' will still be with us. This is neither to idealise the modern state nor to imply that its present functions should be left undisturbed. On the contrary, they should constantly be questioned and reviewed. For just as no particular form of government, no political programme and no political party can be presented as *the* working through of the divine will, so no specific package of governmental responsibilities is definitively ordained by Scripture. (Which is not for a moment to suggest that the Christian citizen has nothing to say about what the tasks of government should be at any particular time.)[12] It is clear enough that the years ahead will be fertile in controversy over where the public/private boundary should be drawn in matters as varied as medical care, education, racial and sexual discrimination, parental rights, pornography, industrial relations – to mention but a few.

While we cannot foresee the detailed outcome of these several battles, doubtless in some the boundaries will shift one way and in some the other. The precise points at which they are eventually drawn may be less important than the fact that there are boundaries. Unlike totalitarian thought systems, which dehumanise men and women by treating them as entirely social creatures, Christianity and democracy in their different ways see man as a private as well as a social being. This recognition is essential to the ability to preach the Gospel and worship freely, and to much else that is precious besides. The dangers of endlessly accumulating state activities do exist, but they are not inherent in large-scale government. The way to 2000 AD does not lead remorselessly to some omniscient, omnipresent state – Hayek's 'road to serfdom' – partly because of the terrible practical lessons of Auschwitz, the Gulag Archipeligo and the Great Proletarian Cultural Revolution, and partly because of the prophetic warnings of writers as diverse as Hayek and Orwell, and churchmen as varied as Archbishop William Temple and Bishops Hensley Henson and George Bell.[13]

In practical terms 'big government' will certainly be with us in the year 2000. Such varied factors as the consequences of the extension of the franchise, the way in which almost every home has a substantial stake in public benefits, the increase in the size and complexity of other social organisations, population growth and the continuing climate of threat in international affairs have all exercised an inherently expansive effect on the tasks of government and the agenda of politics. Cumulatively, such considerations make any really substantial winding down of the scale of state activity unlikely. Even the exceptionally strong-minded efforts of President Reagan to 'get the government off the back of the American people', and of Margaret Thatcher to roll back public expenditure as a way of both invigorating the economy and enhancing personal freedom seem unlikely to produce more than a marginal reduction in state activity.

Yet the difficulties of 'big government' will be manifold. Finance is simply the most obvious problem. In Britain (and much of the ensuing discussion will be illustrated from British experience), the thirty years or so after World War II were marked by increasing public expenditure, which was financed partly from growth, partly from consuming rather than investing, and partly from higher taxation. These were the years when Harold Macmillan promised to double the standard of living in a generation, while Anthony Crosland saw a more just society emerging from an ambitious provision of public services financed by sustained growth. The scale of improvements in the living standards of ordinary people over those years must be recognised and celebrated; these were quite considerable achievements for which the political system too rarely receives its share of the credit. But there were costs too: the social injustices left intact, the loyalties and solidarities destroyed among the victims of change, and the extent to which the West achieved its unprecedented prosperity on the backs of the Third World. But growth has flagged, and the limits of acceptable taxation seem to have been reached. (Britain was by no means at the top of the international tax league, but by the late seventies even many politicians of the Left had concluded that taxation could be pushed no further. Doubtless some of the opposition to higher taxes was purely selfish. But it also reflected popular scepticism about the efficacy of much public expenditure and about the equity of the tax system, which often bore most harshly on the least affluent.) With the crumbling of the Macmillan and Crosland visions, there is now no corresponding confident and influential secular guide to the politics of economic stagnation and mass unemployment which now confront us. The political battles of the nineties will doubtless differ in many important respects from those we know and anguish over today. It would be pleasant to be able to provide a detailed prospective with chapter and verse. But Mendès-France's maxim of *gouverner, c'est prévoir* is peculiarly difficult to apply to government itself. If one considers the confident certainties about the capacity of the economy to finance policies requiring sustained growth, the structure and stability of the 'two-party system', the integrity of the United Kingdom, electoral loyalties and class relationships on which most forecasts of twenty years ago were based, it is clear that detailed futurology is a task for the brave or the rash. In Britain at least, the political future has rarely seemed more problematical. Assuming the continuation of something like conventional politics (i.e. the absence of any major trauma like nuclear war), nobody can now be certain whether in 2000 AD the United Kingdom will still be united, whether it will still be 'in Europe', whether there will be one parliamentary chamber or two, what the electoral system will be, or whether there will be two, three, four (or more) major political parties. And if all these mooted reforms of the political system do come about, we cannot be sure whether their net effect will be dramatic or yet another instance of *plus ça change* . . . Nor can we anticipate the issues on the political agenda in anything more than the broadest terms. We may be reasonably confident that the experience of inflation, depression, urban decay and racial discrimination – to mention just four problems among many – will lay their mark on the political attitudes of the present generation, just as the General Strike and an earlier depression scarred British politics for decades afterwards.

But we cannot foresee in useful detail how current experience of relative failure and deprivation will work through, and we would be unwise to expect history to repeat itself exactly. However, in the shorter run there is little doubt that the extent to which flagging economic performance will constrain political life over the years ahead has still not been fully assimilated. The politics of economic stagnation are likely to be difficult, controversial and divisive.

But then political reality is frequently unappealing and intractable. Human societies have always been diverse. But, quite apart from the implications of the scale and complexity of modern social organisation, prevailing liberal-democratic values favour full expression of that diversity (for both better and worse), whereas earlier forms of political system often denied or stifled it. Where there are clashes of values or interests, many of which will be entirely respectable, Christians with their biblical understanding of the fallen nature of man, should find it far less perplexing than others if these clashes take an anti-social form or are irreducible through the processes of rational argument. In all circumstances our first responsibility is to confront reality unflinchingly, however deeply we may wish that it were different. Bishop Butler is said to have observed: 'Things and actions are what they are, and their consequences will be what they will be. Why, then, should we desire to be deceived?' This I take to be less the somewhat fatalistic acceptance of the status quo that it might appear to be at first glance, than an insistence that the starting point for political action must be a total honesty about the situation and the likely outcome of our behaviour. This is self-evident, perhaps, but I would venture to say that the widespread sense of political disappointment in Britain during recent years has owed far more to the ingrained over-optimism of politicians about their ability to bring about significant change, than to wilful deception on their part.[14]

There are really only two broad approaches to the dilemmas inherent in social diversity: conflict or consensus. Naturally neither is ideal or universally applicable. Consensus may be more instinctively appealing, until one realises that it is attained largely through bargaining and compromise. Compromise – for reasons one can well understand – has a muddied reputation. In many people's minds it has become a synonym for craven or cynical expediency. And sometimes indeed it may be. Perhaps it is precisely because Christians often concentrate their political attentions on a few deeply felt issues, that they tend to overlook the fact that the great majority of political problems have no clearly identifiable 'Christian' solution and raise no particular issues of moral principle. Among the minority of issues that do, we may often find that the choice is not neatly between 'good' and 'bad', but between two positive values which cannot be wholly satisfied. For example, which should prevail, the prosperity of the coal-mining industry together with more secure energy supplies, or the preservation of the beautiful Vale of Bevoir? the traditional culture of the Eskimo whale-hunters of Alaska or the protection of a threatened species? the survival of the Welsh language or the wishes of English parents? For every issue such as abortion, the death penalty or nuclear warfare on which Christians may feel impelled to take an absolute stand, there are a hundred over which they may reasonably differ, where bargaining and compromise represent an honourable and necessary way of conducting the affairs of a divided society. (That even an honourable compromise can be dishonourably conducted should go without saying; there is obviously a world of difference between principled compromise and sheer expediency.)

To suggest, as Peter Hinchliff has done, that perhaps 'the function of Christianity in politics is precisely to be uncompromising' is both to misunderstand the agenda of politics and to adopt an ultimately destructive stance towards the political system.[15] The problem is not whether compromise is necessary, but to identify those situations where it is necessary and proper and those where it is not. To be sure, the game of compromise is often played badly or to excess. For instance, it could reasonably be argued that, in their attempt to obtain the voluntary cooperation of the tobacco industry in restricting cigarette advertising, successive British governments have paid an unacceptably deadly price in delay and ineffectuality. But there are many times where it is right to settle for something less than total victory, either on the principle that half a loaf is better than none, with the hope of returning for more later, or in order to ensure that a policy is widely enough accepted to work. We may wish to double aid to the Third World; it will be something to increase it by a significant percentage. We may believe that the herbicide 2,4,5-T should be banned, but we may have to settle for either greater restrictions on its use or a delay in phasing it out. We may be totally opposed to abortion, but if the political realities are against us for the moment, we may prefer to achieve what we can for the time being by (say) limiting the stage of pregnancy within which it is permissible, than to countenance a more or less totally 'open' situation. (However, many would be morally disturbed by schemes which in effect allowed abortion for the well-off, while closing it to the poor.)

It may seem strange to move from a principled defence of compromise to a commendation of intransigence. Yet precisely because the ways of Christ are not the ways of the world, Christians should also be the last people to shrink *a priori* from conflict. The producer of a recent television talk show remarked that in selecting potential contributors, she mentally dubbed Trotskyists and nuclear disarmers as 'hard' and spokesmen for the churches as 'soft'. Who is to say that she was wrong, or to reject the condemnation implicit in her assessment? It is certainly in keeping with another recent reflection by the Bishop of London: 'The Church today, having lost her nerve, shows at times an almost pathetic desire to be loved by the world.'[16] If it is really true, as Walter James has suggested, that few Christian leaders (and only leaders?) wish to go against the grain of contemporary political assumptions, then indeed the salt has lost its savour. For there will be times when the proper Christian course will be to act in ways which many of our fellow citizens will consider divisive – as indeed they will be!

We must of course be careful that the ground is firm beneath our feet. As Bishop Headlam remarked, 'many good Christians are not only eager to take part in political life that they may help others, . . . but are inclined to identify the particular action which they support with the teaching of Christianity.'[17] Or, as Daniel Jenkins puts it, 'it is never enough for those who believe their cause is righteous to conclude that this conviction legitimises their use of power.'[18] The duty of care we owe to the fabric of the political order makes it doubly important that we think carefully and prayerfully about when to stand firm on principle precisely because we will be doing it in the name of the Gospel. (But beware of the tendency in political arguments to describe every strong disagreement as a matter of 'principle'). We must be quite sure that we are acting solely through a conscience set free in Jesus Christ.[19] If such is the case, then we have no choice, particularly if we accept Karl Barth's view that the prophetic role of the Church encompasses a duty to witness to the state, which is so imperative that indifference would amount to a rebellion against the ordinance of God (Rom. 13.2) – as well as leaving suffering humanity in the lurch.[20]

My main concern here, however, is not the policies as such, but with the political system through which public policy has to be enacted and implemented, especially during a period when the politics of economic stagnation may entail considerable social and political conflict. Society never lacks antagonists. So while there will indeed be times to stand on principle, particularly in the defence of the weak, more than ever there will be a need for 'ministers of reconciliation'. It is strange how readily that phrase is taken to invoke an attitude of woolly-minded moralising or vacillating fence-sitting. For critical involvement outside the warring camps is never easy. The deeper the conflict, the more uncomfortable and the more necessary that stance will be. Nowhere has this been more movingly clear in recent years, than in the sacrificial work of reconciliation by many Christians in Northern Ireland over the past decade or so.[21] Or consider the pain in Basil Moss's retrospect on six years as Chairman of Birmingham Community Relations Council: 'for those of us who get involved it means acceptance of a "can't win" situation, in which one is hated, or regarded as useless or impotent, by the extremists on both sides.' But this must be accepted because God's redemptive love provides the imperative 'both for evangelism, worship, and also for compassion – the compassion which drives us to act as best we may in the social and political scene in the name of that justice, love, patience, and affirmation of the "other" which have their roots in the very being of God himself.'[22]

Earlier contributors to this book have produced an array of prescriptions requiring political power for their implementation. Power was ordained by God for the ruling and ordering of the world. Without it government becomes impossible. Power can be the means of achieving great practical good. Every public good we have won, or hope to win, and many of the most precious private goods we wish to preserve, depend at first or second hand on the actual or potential exercise of political power. But power can be corrupted by selfish aims, by becoming an end in itself, by being exercised unchecked, or by being deployed in the vain glorious illusion that it is the means of applying final solutions to social problems. While all human institutions fall short of the glory of God, there is always more to be said than that if we are to hold any meaningful discussion of social organisation. There are ample biblical precedents for distinguishing between governments which are relatively good or bad. Paul, for example, commends the Roman government of his day (Rom. 13.1–6), though nobody knew its failings better; it provided a reasonably just framework of law within which freedom, good conduct and the preaching of the Gospel were possible, and where the Christians could 'lead a quiet and peaceable life in all godliness and honesty' (1 Tim. 2.2). What a different picture from the 'demonic government' characterised by the 'beast from the abyss' in the Apocalypse (Rev. 130) where power was being employed oppressively and unjustly in the service of absolutism!

As that example underlines, the Christian commitment to any particular regime, however beneficial, will always be contingent, never definitive or permanent. Dr Edward Norman has rightly criticised the tendency to speak as if contemporary liberal-democracy were the embodiment of Christian values.[23] It is not. As T. S. Eliot noted, 'To identify any particular form of government with Christianity is a dangerous error.'[24] At the same time, Barth was surely correct in holding that 'there is clearly no cause for the Church to act as though it lived, in relation to the State, in a night in which all cats are grey.'[25] His own conclusion, after much Christ-centered reflection, was that 'we are justified, from the point of view of exegesis, in regarding the "democratic conception of the State" as a justifiable expansion of the thought of the New Testament.'[26] In the same spirit as that in which Paul commended the Roman government of his day, the virtues of liberal democracy must be recognised and prized – without ever forgetting the manifold injustices which it too comfortably countenances. This is a form of government under which it is possible to 'do good', to worship God, and which in practical terms is reasonably congruent with the diversity of modern society. Critical of it though we may be, we should never cease to give thanks that – at least in most countries of the western world – we live under a government which exercises its power relatively humanely, justly and efficiently.

It is as certain as anything humanly can be that in 2000 AD some 5000 million people will be living under governments which bear little resemblance to that acceptable Roman model. Perhaps only a few will experience 'demonic governments' like those of Hitler and Stalin, Amin and Bokassa, whose rulers 'grind the heads of the poor into the earth and thrust the humble out of the way' (Amos 2:.7); 'who make justice hateful and wrest it from its straight course, building Zion in bloodshed and Jerusalem in iniquity' (Mic. 3.9). Many more, however, will be under regimes which are far from constituting a 'just, participatory and self-sustaining political order' (to employ a formula of the World Council of Churches). Some, in South Africa and the Americas particularly, are a special challenge because they claim to defend 'Christian values' and cloak their repressive rule in what purports to be scriptural legitimation. It is scarcely surprising that Christians inside and outside the authoritarian countries have sometimes fumbled or stumbled in seeking appropriate theological and practical responses to unjust rule. Some have been highly vocal about South Africa and Chile, but mute about Vietnam and Albania (or vice versa). Others have exhausted their energies in token 'demos' and boycotts, rather than in more demanding forms of witness, while others have too readily accepted fashionable 'liberationist' theologies. And some have not been alert enough to the danger, so amply illustrated by history, that today's victims and adversaries of oppression may prove even more oppressive in power. The task of working through our duty to both God and an unjust Caesar will be no easier in the years ahead than it has ever been – and no less necessary. Those wrestling with these problems must naturally be challenged if they fall into error, but one hopes that this may be done with a greater measure of compassionate understanding of their situation than they have sometimes received from fellow Christians.[27]

There are clearly many countries where the bases for a 'just, participatory and self-sustaining political order' do not exist. It is fashionable to blame this on the behaviour of the more developed countries. It is of course not quite as simple as that. Many of the more oppressive states (especially those of Eastern Europe) have no such excuse, while in others there are internal responsibilities for which the West cannot fairly be made the whipping boy. But there is also an important element of truth, and it is preferable to heed that painful thrust of truth than to let awareness of other responsibilities to cushion us from our own. However unwittingly we have exported social and economic modernisation, unemployment and inflation, we have had a part in the destabilising effects of violent fluctuations in the international commodity markets. And there is at least a plausible case that the price of avoiding the ultimate superpower confrontation has been the diversion of rivalries into Third World countries (Korea, Vietnam, Angola, Somalia), where they are conducted over the bleeding bodies of governments and societies. There are plenty of well-meaning voices alerting us to the *economic* implications of our behaviour for the Third World; the *political* cost is much less frequently grasped. But, irrespective of 'blame', the harsh fact is that in the year 2000 countless millions of people will still be living under regimes so poor that they cannot hope to have more than a minimal political effectiveness. Whatever the qualities of their rulers – and post-independence Africa has been blessed with a number of political leaders of remarkable stature – governments can achieve little where there is no administration worth the name, and where their writ may be limited to a few major centres of population. Nor can a country like Bolivia hope for significant betterment as long as it is disrupted by a coup every few months. (With its 200 or so coups since independence, Bolivia is an extreme case, but many more countries suffer endemically from what Octavio Paz has called the 'democracy of violence'.) Economic development and political development are interdependent, yet the one creates much more concern than the other.

None of this is to imply that the abuse of power will become less of a problem in the more advanced countries. On the contrary, the battle against oppression is never-ending, whether against traditional abuses, for which the remedies are known if not sure, or against such newer forms as the inhumanity of vast labyrinthine bureaucracies, or against the danger that new technologies may lead to people being more comprehensively monitored and surveyed, and thus more subtly and pervasively unfree, than ever before. Wherever there are risks either of outright misuse of power, or of more indirect corruptions, public or private, Christian voices need to be heard. The more we press for positive governmental action, the more carefully we need to weigh the potential costs in personal and collective freedoms.

The other side of the coin is less familiar: while the misuse of power can be fatal to freedom, so may its absence. Again, although I am taking the developed world as my primary brief, in many Third World countries the combination of average incomes of under $500 per head and of inadequate structures of government and administration makes it impossible to 'do good' on anything more than a nominal scale. Where the most basic public services are totally lacking, 'freedom' is nothing more than a word. Our problems in the West are as nothing compared with these. All the same, the trends in a number of western societies are worrying. They have long operated on the assumption that once political will has been clarified, the translation into reality is reasonably assured. This has never been absolutely the case, but in recent years there has been a disturbing number of incidents where governments have been unable to attain some of their central policy goals. In Britain incomes policy, industrial relations reform and the chronic failure to achieve targets for economic growth are classic cases in point. Because of the constraints I have already mentioned, such difficulties seem more likely to deepen than to ease in the years ahead.

In a number of western countries the demands on the political system have outrun the capacity for reasonably rapid and effective response. While this is partly related to the shortfall in financial resources, some problems are intractable not because they make particularly heavy demands on the public purse, but because of the load they impose on available political and administrative capacities, or because it is difficult to secure the levels of consent required to make them work adequately. Once more the classic instance is the long search for a workable incomes policy in Britain. The negotiating of the initial agreement may itself be difficult, and may be at the expense of other political choices, whether as a direct consequence of the bargaining process or by claiming the time of senior politicians and administrators that might have been given to other matters. (Time is the scarcest of all political resources.) Once an incomes policy or 'social contract' has been agreed, maintaining its integrity over any substantial period has been highly problematical, because even where there has been support from a majority of the general public, success may be compromised by the actions of relatively small but socially or economically crucial groups like hospital doctors, power workers or firemen. It is easy to castigate these for their selfishness, but the problem is probably inherent in the whole endeavour. Incomes policy is admittedly an unusually difficult area, rather than the norm. Nevertheless, while history is unlikely to repeat itself exactly, the fact that three British governments in less than a decade came to grief in one way or another over relations with the trade unions (and others have found discretion the better part of valour) is something that no forward look can ignore.

While incomes policy is unique in scale, it typifies the way in which, as its tasks have grown, government has been called on to move into areas where the politico-administrative techniques are less proven and perhaps inherently more uncertain than in such traditional functions as building roads, paying retirement pensions or regulating vehicle lighting systems. That is one aspect of the problem. Another is the extent to which large-scale government becomes preoccupied with its own internal coordination. The integrity of government departments becomes compromised as they become bound to sectional groups in terms of information, expertise and ties of mutual obligation. (How many Ministers of Agriculture have earned a reputation as champions of consumer interests?) The danger is partly that government becomes more remote and impersonal to ordinary people, and partly that it gets entangled with interest groups, leaving it more broker than sovereign. What seems at first glance to be a powerful, impregnable centralised government machine, may on closer scrutiny seem more like a disparate archipelago of contending fiefdoms.[28] While I am painting with a brush broadened to the point of caricature, the essential point is simple: in calling on government to do more, we do not necessarily enhance its capacity to respond. It may simply become more thinly spread and less effective.

What concerns me for the future here is the danger of under-performance eroding governmental authority. Democracies are peculiarly dependent on their capacity to command trust, loyalty, consent, obedience or acquiescence commensurate with the tasks in hand, since they are committed to governing with the minimum possible coercion. Governments which cannot achieve their aims by effective popular consent are in danger of collapsing, falling into immobilism or being driven to resort to coercive rule. Each of these options carries threats to freedom.

Authority in largely secularised pluralist democracies, where legitimation by 'divine right' is at best vestigial (though its contribution in Britain and the United States at least is not to be dismissed), is a vulnerable growth which is far easier to erode than to create. It requires constant renewal and reaffirmation. The years ahead promise to be hard for legitimate authority. The 1981 inner-city riots in Britain were one form of warning. One neither excuses them, nor subscribes to any simplistic interpretation of their causes, in saying that they should scarcely have surprised us, since substantial sections of the population – and not simply ethnic minorities – feel themselves outside a political community which appears indifferent to their needs and aspirations. Rioting may not recur; the underlying disaffections will be harder to eradicate. As long as these persist, democracy is under threat from those who consider that their grievances warrant a resort to violence. Democracy may be no less in hazard from those whose response is to demand forms of repression that will undercut the values it purports to defend. There is no surer way of destroying legitimate authority than to defend it by means which dig its grave.

We may be more attuned to such dangers while memories of Brixton and Toxteth linger, but in the longer term there may be subtler (though not less potentially serious) risks of the system becoming locked into a cycle of under-performance, which could leave it incapable of responding to necessary social change. For government inaction can be as great a source of injustice as an overt abuse of power. I think here of the deaths and disease suffered by Neapolitans over the years when the paralysis of Italian government, national and local, prevented the building of a modern sewerage system. Consider, too, the continuing failure of British governments to find satisfactory remedies for victims of abuses of trade union power, to devise an effective machinery for investigating complaints against the police, or to achieve their declared aims of equalising employment opportunities for women. The paradox of modern government is that it can at one moment display a giant's strength; at the next it may be all but impotent.[29]

In a number of countries, pride in the political system was eroded during the seventies. This decline is not entirely explained by events like the Vietnam war or

Watergate, or by disappointment with reformist governments, which may have no parallel in the eighties and
nineties. It would be misleading to assume that such
discontents will remorselessly gather momentum in the
years ahead, though they may in some measure be ineradicable. It has become part of the implicit framework of
political discourse to treat almost every social issue as
potentially susceptible of political resolution. Even some
Christians allow themselves to adopt such optimistic visions at times, for instance by exaggerating the capacity of
laws to 'make men good'. Such optimism loses sight of the
fact that, although there may be a case for ameliorative
measures, the only final and perfect answer to the problems concerning them may lie on a quite different plane
and through Jesus Christ. One of the few themes in Dr
Norman's regrettably negative Reith lectures that truly
struck home was his castigation of the way in which many
Christians have allowed the unique character of their
message to become distorted by fashionable political discourse. This is not, of course, to suggest that Christians
should turn their backs on family break-up, cruelty to
children, world poverty or disarmament. These must be
grappled with on the temporal as well as the spiritual
plane. There is an immense amount to do; the recognition
that the way will be difficult and that perfection is unattainable can never be an excuse for inaction – nor a
reason for pessimism about what can be achieved through
the grace of God.

Christian Social Responsibility in a Pluralist Society
We all have a responsibility to the political order. This is
partly a matter of rendering to Caesar what is Caesar's, of
being as supportive as conscience allows, of praying for
our rulers, and of acting consistently with our prayers. But
it is more than this, more even than being prepared to
think about 'policy'. It includes reflecting on the processes
by which 'policy' will have to be enacted and implemented. It is not enough to say 'there ought to be a

law'; We need to reckon with the full implications of political reality. We have to recognise, for instance, that the system has a limited capacity for conceiving and enacting well-crafted legislation. Every year a number of desirable measures fail simply because Parliament, the National Assembly or Congress cannot find time for them. To put it a little simplistically, every Bill pushed onto the agenda will push another off. (In principle parliamentary process can be accelerated to increase the output of legislation, but sausage-machine lawmaking brings its own dangers.) This has obvious implications for priorities. Laws must be administered and enforced: is what we want administrable and enforceable? Are the requisite administrative talents and organisation available, or can they be brought into being? How effectively can administrators and enforcement agencies be marshalled for the energetic and faithful execution of the legislator's will? Much will also depend on the degree of support or acquiescence the measure enjoys from interest groups and the wider public. All these points are in a certain sense self-evident, and yet it is surprising how often even politically experienced people neglect or dismiss them, to their eventual discomfiture.[30] It is one thing to prohibit the use of blue asbestos or to require vehicles to be fitted with seat-belts; it is another to make the wearing of seat-belts universal or to eliminate secondary picketing. The classic case remains the American experience of prohibition. (The history of American anti-adultery statutes also merits reflection.) There would be comparable difficulties today in achieving a satisfactory measure of gun control in the United States. On both sides of the Atlantic there is a deep tension between the convictions many Christians hold on abortion and the kind of arrangements that currently appear likely to command sufficient public support to be workable. The list could be extended almost at will.

The implication of all this is emphatically not that Christians should be defeatist, silent or inert when their proposals are likely to run counter to the mood of the day. On the contrary, they must never allow the world to write the agenda for the Church, or accept that what may appear to be entrenched social attitudes are immutable. Not forgetting that they may not have the whole truth, and that their own motives and actions may themselves be mixed, Christians have to fight as hard as they can for the causes they hold just. As John Briggs argues, 'Christian social responsibility in a plural society must involve an attempt to influence that society to give proper respect to true values.'[31] That is, securing our political aims is not to be a matter of capturing the formal structures of decision-making through the various techniques of pressure politics; it entails a much broader struggle to change the thinking of society. To be sure, manipulative politics may achieve its aims. Some of the more 'permissive' legislative changes of the past decade or so were largely the product of energetic lobbying by small but determined groups. Some Christians have been tempted to emulate such methods, politically fighting fire with fire. But apart from the fact that some forms of pressure politics raise serious problems of political ethics, many of the causes to which Christians are most deeply committed are peculiarly dependent for their success on public support and observance, in a way that much of the permissive legislation in the opposite direction was not. Such examples as American prohibition, and the apparently ineradicable corruption associated with the illegal status of off-course betting in a number of American states, underline the point. To win purely formal acceptance of one's proposals, only to have them proved unworkable in practice, can lead backwards rather than forwards, while also weakening the fabric of governmental authority.

Once again, the great majority of political questions raise no such dilemmas. Nevertheless, even in routine matters there is a need to think more carefully than hitherto about how much the political system can cope with, and about the qualitative aspects of implementation. In a modern democracy Christian responsibility goes well beyond the submissive law-abiding behaviour appropriate under the Roman empire. We are not mere subjects but, however fractionally, citizen-rulers. Christians still have not altogether come to terms with this either theologically or behaviourally.[32] Harvey Cox is surely right in remarking that 'in the modern church too little is said about the stewardship of power'.[33] This is not to suggest that all Christians are obliged to immerse themselves in practical politics. But to the extent that they do think or act politically, they can and should adopt an understanding, constructive and caring relationship to government. Too often government is taken for granted; like any human institution it thrives only if it is cared for, nurtured and edified.

This is not a matter of being uncritically or unconditionally supportive. Although the general presumption will be that our efforts will sustain and enhance governmental authority (Rom. 13.1–6), precisely because the state 'does not and cannot believe the Gospel', there is a constant challenge to it in the Gospel which we may at times be called to embody.[34] There is much to be learned from the trial of Jesus (which was both an act of governmental power and an abdication of that power). Summoned to that travesty of justice, he submitted to the temporal authority of Rome, meeting it with the searing response of truth and justice.[35] We in turn must pick up that challenge, while recognising that politics is invariably finite and fallible. Thus, while wrongdoers must be punished, and this may entail (say) longer prison sentences, we also know that these are not 'the answer' in any final sense to the problem of law and order. Most of us have every reason to be thankful for the great expansion of educational provision over the past century or so. Yet the fact that this has not 'made men good', as some Victorian optimists hoped, will neither surprise nor discourage us. If unemployment can be brought down to the levels of the fifties, it will be a matter for rejoicing, even if the pathological social behaviour sometimes attributed to unemployment does not disappear with it.

While the theological sense is the more important one in which government is limited, at a strictly practical level it should be clear by now that there are many things that government does not do well; its actions may even be counterproductive. The record of British governments in spotting dynamic new industries to back, or in supporting flagging regions, has been uneven, to say the least. The resources wasted or diverted from other public and private opportunities have been formidable. It is doubtful whether any of the varied attempts, which British governments have made to invigorate the economy after decades of underperformance, have made more than marginal differences either way – perhaps because the problem is insoluble by political means. There is by now abundant documentation of the extent to which welfare measures introduced to aid the underprivileged have in the event disproportionately helped the middle class. (The point is not that there is anything undesirable about helping the middle class, but that the 'target' beneficiaries received much less help than was intended.) Other schemes to help the poor have ended by locking some of them inextricably into a series of 'poverty traps'. In a rather different vein, Bill Jordan has described with telling passion how well-meaning social measures, implemented through large-scale bureaucracies, may deprive people of their dignity, their responsibility, even their identity.[36] Again, most of us will know public institutions which are run more in the interests of their staff than those they were established to serve. The whole cycle of postwar public housing policy in Britain and parts of the United States, with its grandiose slum-clearance projects, the destruction of vital communities, to give way to vast, anonymous high-rise schemes which were to become the new ghettoes or slums of the seventies before, in some cases, being demolished in the eighties, is another cautionary tale which has led some to conclude that political solutions not infrequently become political problems.

Such pessimistic assessments have more than a grain of truth. But they are not the whole picture. For the state which liberated the slaves on both sides of the Atlantic (and how else would they have been emancipated than by dedicated political action?), retains its capacity to liberate from newer slaveries. It is still possible for latter-day Wilberforces to challenge injustice, and triumph. Not that all worthwhile causes will be as grand as that. Here is just a handful of small, uncontroversial examples of effective political action: compensation for vaccine-damaged children, cleaner air and the lessening of noise pollution, the eradication of smallpox, improved vehicle safety standards, more effective control of the dumping of toxic wastes, and the liberation of a number of Soviet dissidents. While none of these is a distinctively 'Christian' cause, that is no reason why we should not celebrate them and learn from them. But the potential will only be achieved if the problems of making the system produce desired results, which have been sketched out here, are recognised and overcome, rather than evaded or denied.

The demand for public intervention will remain high, but the financial, administrative and political resources to meet it will be limited. If the state assumes more functions, it may have to shed others in order to cope, or accept that everything will be done less well. Either way involves awkward choices. To give just one example: in the year 2000 Britain, in common with many other western countries, will have more people of 75 and over than at any previous moment in her history. Now the very old have distinctive needs in housing, medical services and the like. In more affluent times we might have met their needs by ambitious programmes of public expenditure, financed by the increment of growth. That option is currently closed. Should the problem be left entirely to individuals? Or is it entirely a public responsibility, requiring an effort to persuade people to accept higher taxes? Or should there be a switch of resources from some other activity? Even for a sector of the population which attracts public sympathy, as the elderly do, at least in principle, it will not be easy to win acceptance for higher taxes, while nobody would underestimate the difficulties of (say) converting pediatricians into geriatric specialists and maternity wards into old peoples' homes (to state the alternatives in admittedly simplistic terms).

A Call for More Mature Politics

We need to think hard about whether such issues are best tackled by private action, by publicly-aided and monitored voluntarism, or wholly by state agencies. There are some areas where voluntarism will be preferable, others which are best handled by the state: to discover these is not easy, and will require us to rethink some established attitudes.

This is not to idealise voluntarism, or to forget the historical reasons which led the state to assume responsibility for many matters which hitherto had been discharged by volunteers, including the churches.[37] Nor should voluntarism be seen as a cheap approach for hard times, or in any sense an easy way of tackling the problems we are discussing. However, as we look forward to a period when personal leisure seems certain to increase through shorter working hours, earlier retirement and unemployment, it will be a tragic waste if we are incapable of giving scope for some of the energies and talents thus released in forms of collective caring. 'The challenge of leisure' is very much a challenge to our political and social institutions, and particularly to the 'caring professions'. Obviously these problems cannot be unravelled within a necessarily brief discussion; we can simply note them as points where there will be a need for an informed Christian view, not just about aims but also about the political-administrative means by which these can best be promoted.

The years ahead call for a more mature form of politics

than that to which we are accustomed. Any form of adversary politics is likely to entail some oversimplification and exaggeration, and we should not allow ourselves to attach too much significance to this. But anyone who observes the 'political game' charitably and with a full recognition of the fallibility of man and must still find himself asking, 'Is this really the best we can do?' It is fashionable to blame 'the politicians', but the media, the pressure groups and the ordinary citizens who contribute to a climate of excessive and contradictory expectations must share the responsibility. More than a century after Robert Lowe's renowned (and much misquoted) call to 'compel our future masters to learn their letters', levels of political literacy remain desperately low. For that matter, we have a very long way to go before even the most 'democratic' societies fully come to terms with their own democratic ideals.

Not of course that we pin our faith to better political education, greater participation, or new political parties. To do so would imply an optimistic populism which has no place in a Christian understanding of society (Cf. especially Matt. 27. 20–33)[38] But precisely because rulers will at times betray their trust, and because rather too many of the more assertive groups in our society – professional bodies, trade associations and labour unions to the fore – tend to promote the interests of the relatively privileged, political education and participation need to be spread more widely. The resulting educated democracy may well be even more difficult to govern, and authority be more difficult to sustain. That danger must be accepted, for the consequences of having substantial sections of society seeing themselves as politically impotent or outcasts may in the longer term be more dangerous still. I mean no hint of 'that moralistic attitude which requires that everyone should be involved in the great issues of the day', but rather the belief that justice requires that as many as possible should feel potentially capable of making their voices effectively heard.[39] To be sure, Christians have a responsibility to see that the case of the weak and the voiceless does not go by default, but in the longer run the capabilities of even the best-intentioned proxies are limited.

In acting politically, we must be as wary of collective as of individual selfishness. We must beware of self-righteousness, and of claiming to express the Christian view when we really ought to be saying 'I think'. And we must always be concerned to advance our causes by means which edify the political system rather than degrade it. I have in mind those who proclaim their Christian identity in Northern Ireland affairs but who threaten to make the province 'ungovernable', and whose message betrays no hint that God is a God of love. I think, too, of that element in the American Moral Majority movement which, again in the name of Christ, is prepared to take a politician's position on the Panama Canal Treaty as one of the elements in deciding whether he is fit to stay in public life. Precisely because the belief that 'politics is a dirty business' is so popularly engrained, Christians in public life have a special responsibility to demonstrate that the opposite can be true. (And there is similar duty for those who comment on public life to note how many politically active Christians do honour their Lord, not least those who have resisted the sundering of communities in Northern Ireland and have come closer to each other in love and suffering.)

'Protecting the weak' encompasses not just those who are fashionably and sentimentally held to be weak but also the unfashionable weak. Britain commits to prison a higher proportion of her population than any of her neighbours. This alone gives cause for hard thought. But when many of those prisons are, on the admission of one governor, 'human dustbins' where rehabilitation is all but impossible, and the Board of Visitors of another great prison has declared conditions there 'intolerable' at certain seasons, this is an affront to both logic and conscience. We must not fear to say so or to act accordingly, or to meet the charge of being more concerned with aggressors than with victims – as if it were impossible to care deeply about both. As Peter Hinchliff says, protest against injustice 'can be a very lonely and frightening thing' – but there our duty may lie.[40]

The preceding reflections suggest rather an attitude and an approach to problems than firm solutions. Given the argument about the restricted and fallible character of political activity, it could scarcely be otherwise. In the eighties and nineties democracy and authority, where they exist, will be under challenge, though the specific forms of the challenge will differ from one society to another. Individually and collectively, Christians will have to wrestle with these problems, doubtless with great difficulty and very imperfectly. It has been the argument here that they will be obliged not only to ponder what policies to support, but also to confront the reality of politics with all its uncertainties, ambiguities, imperfections – and opportunities. Certainly the political system is finite; it cannot be misused with impunity, and it has to be respected and edified. This will be demanding and difficult, but it is not something on which we can turn our backs – for that cannot be a proper Christian response to anything that happens in this world. Whether as simple occasional voters, or as people who are intensely involved, we all have some responsibility for the welfare of our political system, which we hold in stewardship. We should do so, with serenity, like Abraham 'looking forward to the city with firm foundations, whose architect and builder is God' (Heb. 11.10). Whatever else the eighties and nineties will be, they will be years of political change. Karl Barth reminds us that, for Christians, the greatest of all changes has already occurred. We are the heralds and inheritors of that change. 'When political conditions change, Christians will simply take it as an occasion . . . to rediscover how dangerously and how beneficially, how consistently and how gently, how profoundly and how practically, the Word of God speaks to those who know it is their only refuge.'[41]

Professor Harrison wishes to thank John Briggs and Jeremy Moon for their comments on earlier drafts of his lecture.

1 In D. F. Wright (ed.), *Essays in Evangelical Social Ethics* (Paternoster Press, Exeter, 1981), p. 99.
2 ibid., p. 91.
3 In C. Elliott et al, *Christian Faith and Political Hopes: A Reply to E. R. Norman* (Epworth Press, London, 1979), p. 30.
4 A. Storkey, *A Christian Social Perspective* (Inter-Varsity Press, Leicester, 1979), p. 299. Strictly speaking, use of 'the state' in respect of biblical times is anachronistic; conceptually and empirically 'the state' as we now understand it did not emerge until about the late fourteenth century.
5 L. Mair, *Primitive Government* (Penguin Books, Harmondsworth, 1962), pp. 77, 85 and passim.
6 D. Bonhoeffer, *No Rusty Swords* (Collins, London, 1965), p. 165.
7 Although 'institutionalised injustice' has been stigmatised as a deplorable example of 'secular moralism', injustice can be impersonal (unlike sin), and I find no better way of characterising situations like that in South Africa where an inhumane set of relationships is embodied in an elaborate structure of law, including the constitution. Cf. J. W. de Gruchy, 'Bonhoeffer, Calvinism and Civil Disobedience in South Africa', *Scottish Journal of Theology*, 34(3), 1981, pp. 245–262.
8 See also 1 Cor. 15.24; Phil. 2.9–10; Eph. 1.20–21; 1 Pet. 3.22; Col. 2.15. These references to 'principalities and powers' may apply, at least in a secondary sense, to earthly rulers or structures.
9 Cf. K. Barth, *Church and State* (SCM Press, London, 1939), pp. 62ff for discussion of Christian responsibility to intercede for the state and its rulers.
10 H. H. Henson, *Christian Morality, Natural, Developing, Final* (Clarendon Press, Oxford, 1936), p. 246.
11 ibid., p. 290.
12 Cf. this reflection by Barth: 'Our Church can only comment on political changes according to the particular circumstances. It must refuse absolutely to be tied down to a political line. Only in the rarest cases will its position be the same today as it was fifty or even ten years ago. It remains free simply because it has no other law to proclaim but the law of

Christ which is the gospel. It may have to speak conservative-
ly today and very progressively or even revolutionarily
tomorrow – or vice versa.' *Against The Stream* (SCM Press,
London, 1954), pp. 91–2.

13 Cf. E. R. Norman, *Church and Society in England 1770–1970*
(Clarendon Press, Oxford, 1976), chs. 8 and 9.

14 Thus Harold Wilson has rebutted criticism of his 1964–1970
government by insisting that it fulfilled over 90 per cent of his
party's manifesto commitments. Accepting his contention,
this did not prevent many even of his own supporters feeling
that the state of Britain had not improved by as much as the
manifesto had led them to hope. On the tendency towards
over-optimism in democracy see R. Niebuhr, *The Children of
Light and the Children of Darkness* (Nisbet & Co., London,
1945).

15 In Elliott, op. cit., p. 33.

16 G. Ionescu, 'Speaking Notes With the Bishop of London . . .', *Government and Opposition*, Summer, 1982, pp.
351–361. Cf. Lord Ramsey, former Archbishop of Canterbury: The Church 'must never commend itself to the world
by providing what the world would most like to approve.'
(Norman, op. cit., p. 421). No statement on a controversial
issue will please all 'the world'. The danger lies between
trimming by being all things to all men, and merely echoing a
fashionable line whether it be a pro- or anti-establishment
line.

17 Quoted by E. R. Norman, op. cit. p. 332. For example,
Christians understandably yearn for a just and peaceful
world but *qua* Christians they cannot claim any special
insight or authority about the contending merits of differing
approaches to disarmament.

18 Elliott et al, op. cit., p. 69.

19 de Gruchy, loc. cit., paraphrasing Bonhoeffer.

20 K. Barth, *Against the Stream* p. 89. Note also Sir Fred
Catherwood's warning that to leave our fellows 'to secularism
or humanism would be a complete abdication of our responsibility as Christian citizens.' (H. F. R. Catherwood, *The
Christian in Industrial Society*, Tyndale Press, London, 1964,
p. xi.). There are two ways of leaving our fellows to secularism
or humanism: one is sheer inaction; the other is to be vehicles
of it ourselves. As William Temple insisted, Christian thinking about society should begin not with men but with God.

21 E. Gallagher, *Christians in Ulster 1968–1980* (Oxford University Press, Oxford, 1982).

22 K. Jones (ed.), *Living the Faith* (Oxford University Press, Oxford, 1980). He adds: 'The other thing to be perceived is that the demonic face of insensitivity, prejudice, desire to hurt, partisan politics, violence verbal and worse, are not alas, "over there in society". They are all part of the experience of the Church itself.'

23 I use 'liberal democracy' to distinguish from other variants like 'people's democracy', 'totalitarian' or 'authoritarian' democracy, 'single-party democracy' – in short to indicate a complex of liberties and constraints on power normally referred to in western countries as 'democracy' *tout court*. For further discussion see S. E. Finer, *Comparative Government* (Penguin Books, Harmondsworth, 1974).

24 T. S. Eliot, *The Idea of a Christian Society* (Faber, London, 1939), p. 57.

25 K. Barth, *Church and State*, p. 31. See also Niebuhr's 'vindication of democracy', op. cit.

26 ibid., p. 80.

27 See notably E. R. Norman, *Christianity and the World Order* (Oxford University Press, Oxford, 1979). From the substantial relevant literature I note the following contrasting works: E. R. Norman, *Christianity in the Southern Hemisphere* (Clarendon Press, Oxford, 1981); I. Linden, *The Catholic Church and the Struggle for Zimbabwe* (Longman, London, 1980); T. Beeson, *Discretion and Valour: Religious Conditions in Russia and Eastern Europe* (Fontana Books, Glasgow, 1974); B. R. Bociurkiw, *Religion and Atheism in the USSR and Eastern Europe* (Macmillan, London, 1975).

28 See particularly J. J. Richardson and A. G. Jordan, *Governing under Pressure* (Martin Robertson, Oxford, 1979) for an authoritative discussion with a wide range of examples.

29 Ann Robinson, 'The Myth of Central Control', *The Listener*, 11 June 1982.

30 The title of one of the key works on American experience is adequately eloquent: J. Pressman and A. B. Wildavsky, *Implementation: How Great Expectations in Washington are Dashed in Oakland; Or, Why It's Amazing That Federal Programmes Work At All, This Being the Saga of the Economic Development Administration as told by Two Sympathetic Observers Who Seek to Build Morals on a Foundation of Ruined*

Hopes (University of California Press, Berkeley, 1973). Another work crammed with examples from American experience is E. Bardach, *The Implementation Game: What Happens After a Bill Becomes a Law* (MIT Press, Cambridge, Mass and London, 1977).

31 In Wright, op. cit., p. 77.

32 Briefly, democracies in principle assign a special role, however occasional, to 'the people'. If they are in some sense 'rulers', then it seems to follow that biblical teaching about rulers applies also to the people in that role. In particular, behaviour which tends to hamper the people's ability to exercise the role assigned to them arguably amounts to resistance to rightful authority. Many theologians, from traditions which accord a more central role to the state than is customary in Anglo-American political thought, see divine authority as vested in 'the state', but this does not altogether resolve the problem.

33 H. Cox, *The Secular City* (SCM Press, London, 1965), p. 111.

34 H. Willmer in Wright, op. cit., p. 91.

35 See K. Barth, *Church and State*, pp. 20ff for further discussion of these issues in the trial of Jesus.

36 Bill Jordan, *Freedom and the Welfare State* (Routledge, London, 1976).

37 In earlier days the church undertook widespread practical responsibilities in matters like the care of the sick and education. The transfer of these functions to public authorities was perfectly proper. Equally properly, the church has often moved into areas where the state was deficient – the beginnings of the hospice movement being a case in point. But it cannot be the case that the church should cease to be interested in particular activities, when they pass under public control, on pain of being dubbed 'political'. To envisage the social role of the church in terms of what is neglected by public authorities implies a 'church of the gaps', as unacceptable as the idea of a 'God of the gaps' in the controversy over science and religion.

38 See Niebuhr, op. cit., for further discussion.

39 E. R. Norman, *Church and Society* . . ., p. 461.

40 In Elliott et al., op. cit., p. 27.

41 *Against the Stream*, p. 89.

COMPUTERS DOUBLE PROBLEM

COG IN THE MACHINE 136

INTERDEPENDENCE 141

INNOVATION 141F

1940-1970 142F

7 ENEMIES Vf.

PESSIMISM/OPTIMISM Vii

SOCIALIST ACCUSATIONS 3F, 10

AUTHORITY ERRORS 7

SUSPENDING RIGHTS 7F

OUR SOCIETY 10

MARXISM/HUMANISM 10F

RIGHTS 11

GOD GIVES US NOTHING 12

PERSONAL/SOCIAL 9,14

NORTH/SOUTH 14
RICH POOR

WORLD ECONOMIC ORDER 15

NATIONALISM 7, 17F

REFORMATION/REVOLUTION 18

CHANGES OVER TIME 23, 67

WAR IN ISRAEL 35

PACIFISM/JUST WAR 37F COMMON 40F 61
GROUND

OUR INSECURITY 41F

DECISIONS 60

FALL 62

INTENSIONS/CONSEQUENCES 67

TACTICAL

COMMUNISM + WEST 67